A Theft in Time:
Timedetectors II

For Mom, Dad, and Bill

Tasmania, located in the Southern Hemisphere, experiences the opposite season from the Northern Hemisphere. Summer in the Northern Hemisphere is June through August, while summer in the Southern Hemisphere is December through February. Because of this, the new school year in Tasmania begins just after the new calendar year.

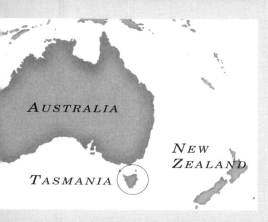

TASMANIA

AUSTRALIA

NEW ZEALAND

TASMANIA

Devonport
Asbestos Ranges • • Beaconsfield
• LAUNCESTON

• Franklin River
• Frenchman's Cap

• HOBART

NDIAN OCEAN

TASMAN SEA

Contents

Remembering the Future

It was just after the New Year. I was sitting on my bed feeling weak and miserable when Mom came in. "Still cleaning out your den, Tom?"

"Yes, Mom," I said. "Nothing else to do."

If I'd said that a couple of years back, Mom would have told me to stop moaning and go bike riding or swimming. Today she sat down beside me.

"You could go fishing," said Mom.

I thought about getting out my fishing things and digging for bait. I thought about baiting my hook. The way I felt, I'd probably drop the bait and stick the hook in my thumb. It all seemed like too much trouble.

"I'll pass today, Mom," I said. "Maybe tomorrow."

Mom sighed. We both knew it wouldn't happen. If you'd told me a year ago that I'd turn down a fishing trip to clean my room, I'd have laughed. A lot can change in a year.

Mom went out, and I started sorting through the box from under my bed. It was full of old jigsaw puzzles, odd socks, a stamp collection, a crash helmet, and the rollerblades I got when I was eleven. I wouldn't be skating this summer, so I tossed the rollerblades into a heap of other stuff. Someone else might as well have them, and I didn't want to be reminded of the things I couldn't do.

I started trying to fit some of the jigsaw puzzle pieces together, but my hands were unsteady. Angrily, I scooped the pieces into the heap. Things were getting worse. Now I couldn't even do a puzzle meant for a nine-year-old.

I put my hands on my knees to keep them from shaking. I was really scared.

I'd been feeling weak for months. I couldn't even remember exactly when it started, because it had come on gradually. First, I got pins and needles in my hands and feet. Then I started getting clumsy.

"Your center of gravity must be changing," Mom said. "You're heading for another growth spurt."

I didn't have a growth spurt, though. As a matter of fact, I didn't grow at all. I'd been feeling bad for about four months when I realized it wasn't going to go away. In fact, it was getting worse. Mom and Dad took me to see Dr. Sands.

"I haven't grown," I said. "I can't even play football anymore. I can't do anything."

The doctor examined me and said I was fine. "Cheer up, Tom," he said. "Make sure you get enough sleep and exercise, and soon you'll be right as rain."

I did as he said, but I got worse, so Dr. Sands sent me to the hospital for some tests. I won't tell you about that. It was boring and uncomfortable, and it didn't do any good at all.

I spent most of the year having tests and feeling worse and worse. The doctors agreed that I had some weakness in my muscles and nervous system, but they didn't know the cause or the cure. They also didn't seem to think it was serious.

"Try positive thinking, Tom," said Mom. "Imagine yourself feeling better and better."

I tried that, but I just got weaker. And now, in the early summer, I didn't feel like doing anything at all.

Right at the bottom of the stuff I was sorting, I found an old shoe box. Inside were some mangled bits of metal and a gun. It wasn't a normal gun, of course. It was a sol-shot. It looked like a plastic ray gun. It was a dull black, with buttons and a trigger. I thumbed the safety catch off and squeezed the trigger. Nothing happened. I hadn't expected anything to happen, so I laid the sol-shot down on the desk by the window and stared at it for a long time. I was remembering the future.

That's impossible for *most* people, but I could remember the future because I'd been there. That's where I got the sol-shot.

It happened like this.

When we were eleven, my friend Coxie and I went camping in the Asbestos Ranges. Using my dad's metal detector, we found some metal medallions and an opalized skull that was more than 5,000 years old. Scientists thought the skull was a hoax because it looked far too modern to have been buried in the ranges for all those years.

The medallions carried Coxie and me back in time and we met the skull's owner. Her name was Lizba Smith and she was one of the scientists who had invented the medallions. Lizba was from the 32d century – more than a thousand years in our future. In the future, there was great social and environmental upheaval. People were forced to give up all their luxuries – except their pets. Lizba's partner Palmer thought people should get rid of their pets, too. He wanted to use the medallions to travel back in time so he could kidnap or kill a politician named Kane before Kane grew up to defeat Palmer's wishes. Palmer forced Lizba to take him into the past, but she took him too far into the past.

Palmer found Coxie and me with Lizba. He shot me with a sol-shot and kidnapped Coxie.

That might have been the end of us, but Palmer died soon after. I had to use Lizba's sol-shot to destroy her computer so no one else could use her research. Coxie and I got home safely, but Lizba died when she destroyed the medallions we'd used. All we had to remind us were the mangled medallions and Lizba's sol-shot. It didn't work anymore after I'd used it to wreck the computer, so I'd put it away and forgotten it.

So far, that had been the biggest adventure of my life, traveling to the future with Lizba and Coxie, and helping to defeat Palmer's group. The way I felt now, I thought it might be my *only* adventure. I was wrong about that, though. While I sat there, remembering the future, a new adventure was already beginning – an adventure that would take me a long way in time, and closer to death than I like to remember.

Who's Got the Skull?

I closed my eyes, and of course, I went to sleep. I dreamed about Lizba's skull. Lizba had been from the future, but she'd died a long time in the past. Rain and erosion had scattered her bones, and all that was left were the medallions and her skull. You may think of skulls as being funny or scary, but Lizba's skull wasn't like that. It was opalized, and when we found it, I thought Mom might like it for her display cabinet. The police took it, though, and we'd never got it back.

I woke up feeling weak and miserable, and I had a headache. The sol-shot was still on my desk, so I stuck it in my pocket. It was dinnertime. I didn't feel hungry, but I went out to the kitchen.

"Tom, what would you say to a short camping trip?" said Dad.

I thought about camping. I thought about pitching tents, splashing in the creek, and climbing the ranges. I wouldn't be able to have fun. I'd just have to sit near the tent, pretending to enjoy myself. "No thanks, Dad," I said.

"Why not visit Coxie?" suggested Mom.

I thought about Coxie. After the adventure with Lizba we'd sort of drifted apart. Then, Coxie's mom had married Mr. Watts, who used to teach us at school. That was a real surprise, because Mr. Watts ran the Adventurers club, and you never saw anyone who hated adventures more than Coxie's mom. Maybe she'd changed. Anyway, they'd all moved east to Devonport. Coxie had written to me a couple of times, but I hadn't written back, so I couldn't very well ask to stay with them now. Besides, Coxie's mom would make a huge fuss over me. "No thanks," I said.

I saw Mom bite her lip.

"There must be *something* you'd like to do," said Dad. "You can't spend the summer sitting around feeling sorry for yourself."

I thought about it, but there didn't seem to be much of anything I wanted to do, except go to sleep. That was my rock-bottom day. It's pretty rough when you're only thirteen and you're at the end of your rope.

"Tom?" prompted Mom.

"Oh, right," I said. "Dad, you remember that skull Coxie and I found?"

Dad looked astonished. "Who wouldn't remember being interviewed by the police? Not to mention the fuss the newspapers made. What about it, Tom?"

"Do you know who's got it now?"

Dad frowned. "I don't really know. It's probably on display in a museum by now."

"If it were in a museum, we'd have heard," I said. "They'd have to tell us. After all, we found it."

"That's true," said Dad.

"They could at least put a card in the case, saying who found it." I said.

"Maybe," said Dad. "But it might be in the science department at the university, or still with the police. Why the sudden interest, Tom?"

I shrugged. "You mentioned the Asbestos Ranges just now, and that's where we found the skull."

"We could go and see what else we can uncover," said Dad hopefully.

"Come on, Dad," I said. "Everyone's been detecting there since then. There's nothing left to find. Still, I'd really like to know what happened to that skull." I poked at the food on my plate.

"Why don't you try to find out, Tom?" suggested Dad. "Make it your project for the summer."

I started to shake my head. "I can't be…"

"No!" said Mom. "No, Tom Stratton! Don't you dare say you can't be bothered!" She jumped up and grabbed a pencil, a pad, and the cordless telephone and plunked them down in front of me. "Get started," she said tightly. "Start calling and find out who has that skull.

Do it *now*. Insist on being told. It's your moral right to know, and it's *my* moral right to see my son showing a bit of life!"

Dad and I stared. Mom doesn't often blow her stack like that. "Better do as she says, Tom," Dad said, shaking his head, "or it might very well be *your* skull that ends up in a museum."

"Sure," I said. "The boy who wouldn't grow."

Mom left the kitchen in a rush, and Dad started stacking the plates. After he'd gone, I sighed. I knew it would take more energy to resist Mom than it would to do as she said.

First I telephoned the local police department. It took three tries, but in the end I got through to Sergeant Kerry, one of the police officers I'd met before. "This is Tom Stratton," I said, making my voice deep so he'd take me seriously.

"Yes?" Obviously, he didn't have a clue who I was.

"Tom Stratton," I repeated. "I was one of the people who found that opalized skull out in the Asbestos Ranges. It was nearly two years ago. Do you remember?"

"I remember now. What can I do for you, Tom?"

"I want to know who has the skull," I said.

Sergeant Kerry said he didn't know.

"You must know," I said. "You took it. You must know what you did with it."

"We did take custody of it at the time," he said, "but since no crime had been committed, it isn't under our jurisdiction anymore."

"But where is it?"

15

"That's a difficult one." He sounded a bit impatient. He'd probably rather be out solving crimes, but public relations meant he had to be polite to me.

"I need to know," I said, trying to sound firm and responsible.

"Try the university," he said doubtfully. "Or the Yarra Museum. I think they had it at one time."

I thanked him and telephoned the university. They said to try the Yarra Museum. That meant a long-distance call, and I could imagine the dollars adding up on the telephone bill as they passed me from department to department. Finally, I was connected with someone who told me they *had* had the skull. They'd been testing it and investigating it, but a local anthropologist had said they couldn't keep it, because it had been discovered in Tasmania. The anthropologist had threatened legal action if they didn't give it back.

"Do you know his name?" I asked.

"Oh yes," the museum man said sourly. "I know *her* name. Dr. Sylvia Pennyfather."

"I suppose you can't give me her address?" I said.

"I shouldn't," he said, and he gave me her address.

Hot on the Trail
of the Skull

The address was in Devonport, Coxie's new hometown. I couldn't find Dr. Pennyfather's telephone number in the directory, and the operator told me it was unlisted. And no, I couldn't have it, even if it were a matter of life and death.

I decided I would write to Dr. Pennyfather and offer information about the skull in exchange for news on its current whereabouts. I asked her to telephone me.

I waited for more than a week. During that time, I took a long, hard look at myself, and I really didn't like what I saw. I was feeling weak and tired, but surely I could do *something*. So I did do something – real heroic stuff! I took the dog for a walk. It was only two blocks, and when I got home I felt as if I'd run a marathon, but it was better than sitting around.

I went for a walk every day that week. It didn't make me feel better, but it didn't make me feel worse either. All that time, I waited for a reply from Dr. Pennyfather. I really wanted to know what had happened to Lizba's skull. You see, I admired Lizba, because she didn't give up. Even when she was dreadfully injured, Lizba did what she had to do. If I gave up now, I'd be letting her down.

Eventually, I got fed up and decided to go pay a visit to Dr. Pennyfather.

"I'll drive you," said Mom, when I told her my plans.

"Thanks, Mom," I said, "but I'd rather take the bus."

"Are you sure you can manage, Tom?"

"Look, Mom, I'm thirteen," I said reasonably. "I've only got to get on and off the bus, then walk a couple of blocks."

"What if she isn't there?" said Mom. "You'll have a long wait for a bus back home."

"Then I'll go and see Coxie," I said.

Mom nodded reluctantly, then telephoned Coxie's mom, Mrs. Watts, and arranged for me to visit Coxie while I waited for the bus. There was a lot of racket going on in the background, and I could hear Mrs. Watts raising her voice so Mom could hear.

"What was all that?" I asked, when Mom hung up. "It kind of sounded like a chain saw. Or was it that ratbag bird, Cracker?"

19

Cracker is Coxie's cockatoo, and he loves the sound of his own voice.

"That was Coxie's baby sister," said Mom.

I hadn't known Coxie had a baby sister. I couldn't imagine Coxie's mom and Mr. Watts with a baby, especially not a baby that sounded like a chain saw.

"Maybe I won't go after all," I said.

"But you're hot on the trail of the skull! You can't give up now."

"Can't I?" I muttered, but I knew Mom was right. I was committed to finding Lizba's skull. I had another reason for this visit, too. Since anthropologists study the human race, they have to have open minds and be interested in new ideas. Dr. Pennyfather might just know how to cure my muscles.

I put on clean clothes because I wanted to be taken seriously. I also put the sol-shot in my pocket. I'd never shown it to anyone but Coxie, but I thought Dr. Pennyfather might be interested in an artifact from the distant future. Not that I'd tell her it was from the future, exactly. Not unless she seemed open to the idea. At the last minute, I scooped up the mangled remains of the time medallions. They were ruined, but they were made of an unknown alloy, and I thought they'd interest her, too. I was right – in a way. She became interested. *Too* interested! But you can blame a nut named Baz for that.

Mom drove me to the bus stop. "No sense in getting tired before you start," she said. She handed me her mobile phone. "Just in case you need to call Coxie's mom. I wish Dr. Pennyfather knew you were coming."

"Well, the worst she can do is tell me to go away," I said. "And why should she? She's a student of the human race, right? I'm part of the human race!"

"That you are, Tom," said Mom.

I got off the bus in Devonport, and looked around. This was the first time I'd been out on my own for months. (You can't count walking two blocks in your own hometown as going out.) Dr. Pennyfather lived in a cul-de-sac off one of the main streets. Her house was surrounded by high stone walls, and a sign warned me the property was protected by an alarm system.

There was a big wooden gate in the wall, with metal spikes on top and an electronic lock. I knocked, but there was no answer, so I turned to a square intercom set in the wall. There was a sign over it that read DELIVERIES. I was delivering myself and some information, so I pushed the button with my thumb, and after a minute there was a squawk next to my ear: "Hwizzet?"

"I've come about the skull," I said, as slowly and clearly as possible.

There was a loud buzzing sound, and the gate's lock opened.

The Shadow

Dr. Pennyfather came out to meet me. She was short and very ordinary, with piled-up brown hair and a long nose. She looked at me as if I were a flea.

"You're not Dr. Kane!" she said.

"I never said I was."

"You said you'd come about the skull." For a student of the human race, she didn't seem very friendly.

"Yes, I did. My name's Tom Stratton. I wrote to you ten days ago, asking about your plans for the skull."

"I remember," she said, frowning. "Why are you here?"

"I came because you didn't call me."

"Quite so," said Dr. Pennyfather. "I didn't call you, because I didn't want you to come."

"This won't take long," I said. "I really just want to know…"

"You want to know all about my work so you can write some school project," broke in Dr. Pennyfather. She sighed, then continued, "I've heard it all before! I have informed the local school that I am not available for interviews. Now it appears I must inform your school as well. Some people are extremely inconsiderate."

"This has nothing to do with school," I said. "It's about the skull. The Yarra Museum said you had it."

"So?" She raised her eyebrows over squinty little eyes.

"I'd just like to know what you're doing with it," I said. "I was the one who found it, you know." Actually, Coxie was the one who really saw it first, but I didn't want to confuse the issue.

"So?" she said again.

"I *found* it!" I said. "If it hadn't been for Coxie and me, you never would have even seen it! I can give you information you can't get anywhere else."

She gave me a dirty look. "There is nothing you can tell me. Archeology is not a game for amateurs. Untold harm is done every year by unqualified persons doing precisely what you have done. Digging up priceless remains! Handing them over to the police! I'm surprised you didn't play soccer with it!"

I lost my temper. "I know plenty about that skull that you don't know," I said. "I can tell you whose it was, and what she looked like. I can tell you when she was born."

Dr. Pennyfather looked at me coldly. "You are talking nonsense. Get off my property."

"At least let me see it," I said.

"Absolutely not! The specimen is safely packed away. Now leave, before I call the police."

My hands were shaking, so I tucked them into my pockets. I felt tired and dizzy. I hated the thought of Lizba's skull being poked at by this woman. It wasn't dignified and it wasn't right. "Why don't you use this mobile phone to make the call?" I offered. "Tell Sergeant Kerry what you just told me. Ask him if *he* played soccer with the skull." I held out the phone, but she pushed my hand away. "If you're not interested in knowing about the skull's origin, how about these things from the same period?" I pulled out the ruined time medallions from under my handkerchief.

"I am not interested in your pieces of rubbish," she said. "The only interest I have in *you* is in your absence."

"Right!" I said. "I'm going!" I felt like pulling Lizba's sol-shot out of the other pocket and waving it at her. It wouldn't have hurt her (or so I thought), but it would have given her an awful shock. But then she really might have called the police, so I decided to ignore the temptation. As it turned out, that was a good thing!

After Dr. Pennyfather had locked the gate behind me, I stuck out my tongue. So much for her! I leaned against the wall until I felt a bit better, then I set off for Coxie's place, taking a shortcut through the busy mall.

It wasn't very far, but I had to keep stopping to rest. I pretended I was window-shopping. That's how I found

26

out that a man was shadowing me. Every time I stopped, he did, too, and I kept catching his reflection in the store windows. He was wearing a slim-line wet suit, which wasn't as weird as it sounds. There are heaps of good beaches near Devonport. Still, it was an unusual thing to be wearing downtown. I thought I'd seen him before, but I didn't know where. And if he *didn't* know me, why was he following me? Had Dr. Pennyfather sent him to keep on eye on me? That would be crazy, but Dr. Pennyfather did seem a bit odd.

I decided to lose him, but it wasn't so easy. I tried ducking in and out of stores, but he stuck to me like glue. There wasn't much he could do to me in a crowded mall, but I was getting fed up, so I went into the next store and approached the checkout clerk.

"That guy's following me," I said. "The one in the wet suit. See? He's just come in. I think I've seen him before somewhere, but I don't know him. Is there any way I can get out the back?"

"Are you pulling my leg?" asked the clerk.

"Of course not!"

"Our store detective's over there. He'll help you."

"He might not mean any harm," I said.

"Better to be safe than sorry," she said. "Are you all right? You look pale."

"I'm all right," I said. I wasn't, but there was really no use telling her that. The store detective headed off the wet-suit guy, and I went out through the back exit.

I'd lost my shadow, but the funny thing was, I felt more scared than I had before. I even thought about using the mobile phone to call the police, but what could I say? A guy in a wet suit had walked behind me, looking in the store windows? He'd followed me into a store? So what? He hadn't threatened me.

I had an awful cramp in my side, and my legs felt ready to drop off, but I kept on going. Five minutes later, puffing and panting like crazy, I was knocking on Coxie's front door.

The New, Improved Coxie

I almost didn't recognize Coxie. He used to be little and skinny, but now he was a head taller than me, and much wider, too. His floppy hair was the same, but his chin was longer, his nose was bigger, and he had light fuzz on his upper lip. And I'd never had to look up at Coxie before.

"Coxie?" My voice squeaked with surprise.

"Hi, Tom." His voice sounded different, too.

I couldn't tell if he was pleased to see me or not. The old Coxie would have been grinning like crazy. This new, improved version was looking as if I wasn't quite what he'd expected.

"You're bigger," I said.

"You're not," said Coxie.

He said something else, but his voice was drowned by a chainsawing noise from the next room. Coxie made a face. The chainsawing noise was joined by shrieks and squawks and a noise like a wet sheet being shaken in the wind. I followed Coxie into the living room. The noise was even worse in there, but Coxie's mom didn't seem to mind. She was cuddling a bawling baby, and grinning at the cockatoo Cracker, who was hanging upside down from his perch by the window, beating his wings and squawking. Coxie went across and stuck out his arm. Cracker shut up, flipped upright, and waddled up Coxie's arm to his shoulder. That cut the noise level by half.

"Tom's here!" yelled Coxie.

His mom smiled at me. "Hello, Tom." She patted the baby's back. There was more bawling, a burp, then silence, except for the ringing in my ears. Then Cracker said something I'd better not repeat.

"That bird," said Coxie's mom. "He starts up every time Nattie does."

"How've you been?" asked Coxie.

"Not so good." I offered my finger to Cracker, but he hissed. He didn't remember me, and I wished I'd brought him an apple.

"What's wrong with you?" asked Coxie.

I shrugged. "I don't know exactly, but I don't think it's catching."

Coxie's mom gave him a warning glance, then said, "It's good to see you, Tom. Any chance of you staying a few days? You and Coxie have some catching up to do."

This time Coxie gave *her* a warning glance. "Tom won't want to hang around the Noise Machine," he said, pointing to the baby. "Anyway, he's probably going camping with his dad."

"Not this year," I said.

"Your mom said you were seeing someone in town, Tom," said Coxie's mom.

"I came to see Dr. Pennyfather, but she didn't like me."

"She doesn't like anyone," said Coxie. "She's just an old bat."

"Coxie," said his mom. "Are you doing a project of some kind, Tom?"

"Not exactly. I'm trying to trace that skull we found. Remember, Coxie?"

After he'd been kidnapped by Palmer, Coxie had tried to forget our time-travel adventure. He'd tried to act as if it had never happened. I expected him to change the subject, but he nodded. "Sure. I've been thinking about that myself. Did you find out anything?"

"Not much," I said. "The police let it go to a museum, but Dr. Pennyfather has it now. I went to see her, but unfortunately, she didn't want to see me."

Coxie's mom laughed. "That's her! Tell Tom what happened when you met her, Coxie."

Coxie shrugged. "I tried to interview her for social studies last year. She wouldn't talk to me though. If I'd known she had the skull, I might have tried a little harder. Did she show you the skull?"

"No way," I said gloomily. "She wouldn't even let me in the house."

"Let me show you the aviary," said Coxie, so we went out to the backyard. Cracker's new home was made

of steel mesh. It had a lot of perches and swings, and both food and water dispensers. It was a lot better than the rickety old cage at Coxie's old place.

"Gee, that's a parrot palace!" I said.

"It's thirty cubic meters," said Coxie proudly. "I'm going to get Cracker a friend as soon as I can afford it."

"Who made the cage?"

"Wattsie and me, mostly," said Coxie.

"Great. What's it like, having your old teacher as your stepdad?"

"Wattsie's all right." Coxie grinned. "The Noise Machine's a pain in the eardrums, but if it was a toss-up between living with Wattsie and the Noise Machine or living with neither of them, I'd take them both, anytime. Mom's so busy now she's given up fussing over me. Open that latch, will you?"

I had to use both hands, and it took ages to work it loose.

"Hurry up," said Coxie. "He's biting my ear. Ow! Cut that out, Cracker!"

"I'm trying," I said.

The door came open and Coxie tossed Cracker onto the nearest perch. The cockatoo gave a big whistle and climbed across to the food dispenser, where he started stuffing sunflower seeds into his beak. Coxie shook his head. "Gee, you're in pretty bad shape, Tom," he said. "Are you always this weak?"

"No," I said. "Sometimes I'm worse."

"Gee," said Coxie again. He really pitied me, and I felt like sinking straight into the ground. Heck, *I* used to feel sorry for Coxie, because of his asthma and his dead dad and brother and his nervous mom. Now Coxie was bigger and stronger. He had a new dad and a sister, and his mom had stopped fussing. Now Coxie was busy feeling sorry for *me*.

"How's your asthma?" I asked.

"Fine," said Coxie. "I grew out of it, I guess."

"Lucky you." I turned away so he wouldn't see how envious I was.

"It's a funny thing, you suddenly wanting to see the skull," said Coxie.

"What's funny about that, Coxie? You said you'd been thinking about the skull, too," I said. "Did you have any reason?"

"Yes," said Coxie. "I think someone's made some more time medallions."

The Wet-Suit Guy

I stared at him. "How could that be? Lizba and I made sure that could never happen. The only medallions were the ones Lizba made, right? They melted when she died. And I destroyed her computer files."

"I know," said Coxie.

"So how *could* there be more? Palmer knew about them, but he died, too."

"Maybe someone went back in time to before they were destroyed," said Coxie.

I laughed. "The only way to time travel is to use the medallions. The only way to get the medallions would be to *use* the medallions, and the only way to use the medallions would be to *get* them. It's the chicken and the egg."

34

"A paradox," said Coxie.

"That's the word." I sat down in a lawn chair. "So how could there be more medallions?"

"I can think of at least two possibilities," said Coxie.

"Well, go on, genius. Amaze me."

"If you're going to be like that, forget it!" Coxie glared at me, and I remembered that we'd disagreed about the medallions once before. That time, I'd punched him. I'd been bigger than him, then. Now he was bigger than me. If he knocked me down now, I didn't think I'd be getting up.

"Sorry, Coxie," I said. "Tell me."

"It's like the difference between safety pins and computers," he said.

"What?"

"Safety pins were invented by one particular person," said Coxie. "We know who, and we know when."

"So?" I said.

"Computers don't have a single inventor," said Coxie. "Lots of people contributed to them. Most things are made by government-funded research teams these days, not by single inventors."

"That's true," I agreed.

"Sometimes," pursued Coxie, "two different teams invent the same thing independently. Boomerangs were used in different countries. The telephone was invented twice, and weren't there lots of Polar explorers at the same time?"

"So, you think someone might have reinvented time medallions, not knowing Lizba had done it already."

35

"It could have been done at any time in the next twelve centuries," said Coxie. "Or it could have been done twenty centuries from now. If Lizba and Palmer could do it, why not someone else?"

I gulped. Time travel sounds like fun. It sounds like a great chance to change history and fix mistakes, but the adventure with Lizba and Palmer taught me what Coxie had known all along. Time travel is very dangerous, for the people traveling and for the people they meet. Time travel can kill you.

"Good point, Coxie," I said.

"It's also possible Lizba's files were copied before you wrecked the computer," said Coxie. "Palmer could have given them to someone."

"Palmer's dead," I said.

"Palmer," said Coxie, "hasn't been born yet. And what about all his friends?"

I groaned. "So, it *could* have been done. What makes you think it *has* been?"

"Well, I think I've seen someone from Lizba's time hanging around in the mall."

That really shook me. Time travelers in the Asbestos Ranges are one thing. Time travelers wandering around the mall are far too close to home. "Oh."

Coxie nodded. "I was down at the mall the other day and I saw this guy in the arcade."

"Was he wearing a wet suit?" I asked.

"That's right. How'd you know?"

"I saw him, too," I said. "In fact, he was following me today."

"Great, just great," said Coxie glumly. "I suppose he followed you here." He shot a look toward the front gate, as if he expected to see the wet-suit guy loitering near the mailbox.

"No, he didn't." I told Coxie how I'd gotten the store detective to intercept the man. "He might be harmless though," I said, "even if he is a time traveler. After all, Lizba didn't mean any harm."

"Lizba did *her* time traveling in the Asbestos Ranges, not the mall," pointed out Coxie.

"Maybe this guy's a time tourist."

"Who just happens to show up here and now? Who just happens to follow you through the mall? Come off it, Tom! That's too coincidental."

"What could he want?"

"I don't know," said Coxie, "but if he's anything like Palmer, he's after more than postcards from the past."

"I suppose so," I said gloomily.

Coxie stuck out his jaw. "We can't just sit around while this wet-suit guy assassinates the prime minister or Lizba's ancestors or…"

"Or what?" I prompted.

Coxie looked embarrassed, and for a few seconds it was like having the old Coxie back – the old Coxie who was afraid of danger.

"Or what?" I repeated.

"Or us," said Coxie. "All right? I don't want to sit around while this wet-suit guy decides to assassinate you and me."

I stared at him. "Why would he?"

37

"Because we know things we shouldn't know," said Coxie. "We know about time travel, and we know about Palmer and what he tried to do to Kane. If we wanted to be really smart, we could put a stop to all that. We could leave a time-delayed message for Lizba so she never teams up with Palmer in the first place. Because of what we know, we could change the future."

"I would if I could," I said, "but there's no way kids like us can get ahold of the technology we'd need."

Coxie sighed. "Right, Tom. But kids like us grow up. And who knows what technology might be available in twenty years? Things are developing all the time."

I looked down at my hands, which were shaking again. "Coxie, I don't think I'm going to live twenty years," I said. "I don't think I'm going to live *two* years."

It was the first time I'd admitted that to anyone, including myself. If I'd known how little time I really did have left, I'd have felt like dying on the spot.

Total Recharge

Coxie looked uncomfortable. "I thought you said the doctors didn't know what was wrong with you."

"They don't, but it's getting worse," I said. "I haven't grown in more than a year, and I feel weak all the time. The doctors don't seem worried, but they don't know how rotten I feel."

Coxie cleared his throat. "I'd better just try to deal with this wet-suit guy by myself."

"What are you going to do?"

"I'll try to find out what he wants," said Coxie, "without being obvious."

"I've still got Lizba's sol-shot," I said, "if that's of any use to you."

Coxie stared. "Gee! Why didn't you say so?"

"You didn't ever want to know. And don't go getting any bright ideas about being a big hero. It doesn't work anymore. The battery pack must be exhausted."

"I don't suppose you've got it with you?" asked Coxie hopefully.

"Yes, I meant to show it to Dr. Pennyfather." I pulled the sol-shot out of my pocket and tossed it to Coxie. But my hand was shaking again, so my throw was a bit off.

The sol-shot bounced on the grass and fired.

There was no bang and no flash. The sol-shots of the future don't make a bang or a flash. What they *do* make is a nasty mess of whatever they happen to hit. When Palmer shot me with one in the 30th century B.C., I was paralyzed from the neck down for awhile. It was horrible, and thawing out was even worse. I don't think I've ever hurt so much! On another setting, sol-shots can be used to melt metal and plastic, or to scramble electronic circuitry. I hadn't bothered with the setting, because I thought it was dead. Only it wasn't.

The ray hit the edge of the aviary, and the mesh glowed. Two links glowed red, then went black, then melted away.

Coxie let out a squawk of dismay. "What'd you do that for? You might have killed Cracker!"

My heart was beating wildly. "But it's been dead for more than a year!" I said. "It's never worked since it melted the medallions and the computer! Honestly, Coxie, I tried it a few days ago and I swear it was as dead as a dinosaur!"

"It isn't dead now!" snapped Coxie.

I shivered. I'd been carrying the sol-shot in my pocket with the safety catch off. I'd thought about waving it at Dr. Pennyfather to give her a scare. If I had done that, I could have killed her, or myself. Just now I could have killed Coxie. And if I had killed Cracker, Coxie never would have forgiven me. I don't know what it is about sulfur-crested cockatoos, but the people who have them say they make the best friends in the world.

Coxie glared, then bent to look at the mesh. Cracker climbed down to look, too, then stuck his beak through the hole. "Get back in there, you ratbag!" said Coxie, shoving him back. "Get some wire and the pliers from the shed, Tom. Quickly! I don't want him to hurt himself on this jagged edge."

I fetched the wire and watched while Coxie quickly wove it in to replace the melted mesh. He didn't look at me again until he'd finished. "Dead as a dinosaur, right?" he said bitterly.

"It was!" I said.

"Then it's had a total recharge," said Coxie. "What'd you do? Plug it into an adapter? Or did you stick in a a couple of batteries?"

"I didn't do anything!" I said. "I found it in a box under my bed, and it's been sitting on my desk for the past week. Just sitting there."

"In the sun?"

"Some of the time."

"It's solar powered," said Coxie. "I'll bet you." He seemed to have simmered down.

"You know I wouldn't risk hurting Cracker," I said, "or you."

Coxie grunted. "Let's put the safety on."

Very carefully, I picked up the sol-shot and pressed the safety. I checked by trying to fire it again, but it was safe now. "I'll drain it later," I told Coxie. "I'll put it back under my bed."

"It's better to get rid of it," said Coxie.

"How? If I throw it away, some kid might find it. Who knows what would happen if I tried to burn it."

Coxie grinned suddenly. "Guess it's like a diaper or nuclear waste," he said.

"*What?*"

"You can't get rid of nuclear waste, and Mom says disposable diapers are practically as bad. You just can't get rid of them." Coxie paused, then added, "Well, come on."

"Where to?"

"The mall," said Coxie. "Let's see if we can find the wet-suit guy."

"All right," I said. "But I warn you, I've about used up my exercise ration for today. You take the sol-shot, Coxie. My hands aren't too good. I'll leave the mobile phone with your mom."

Coxie tucked the sol-shot into his pocket, then stuck his head in the doorway and yelled out to tell his mom we were going down to the mall. In the bad old days, she would have warned him to put on a jacket, wipe his feet, and not talk to strangers. Now, she just said she'd see him later.

"What time's your bus, Tom?" asked Coxie.

"About four," I said.

"Plenty of time then. Got any money?"

I did, so we went down to the mall and bought some sandwiches and fruit juice, then sat down on the edge of the fountain to watch out for time travelers. "What do we do if we *do* see him?" I asked.

"We'd better play dumb," said Coxie. "Convince him that we've practically forgotten all about it. That way he should give up any idea of getting rid of us… I hope."

"Sounds good to me. I wonder if he'll show?"

"I guess he…" Coxie didn't finish. Instead, he sputtered orange juice all over his shirt.

"Can't I take you anywhere without a bib, Coxie?" I said.

Still sputtering, Coxie jerked his head sideways. There, standing right by the fountain, was the wet-suit guy.

He didn't look very threatening. I'd been nervous when he'd followed me earlier, but now that I was with Coxie, it didn't seem so bad.

So, what's the difference between people from the future and ourselves? Not a lot, because twelve or fifteen centuries isn't very long in evolutionary terms. There is something, though. Something. Maybe Dr. Pennyfather could have explained it, if she'd been willing.

I looked at the wet-suit guy for a couple of seconds, then I glanced at Coxie. He was busy cleaning up his shirt. When I looked back, the wet-suit guy was gone.

Conversation with a Time Traveler

"Hey!" I said. "Where did he…"

I stopped because suddenly he flickered back into view. He came toward us, smiling as if we were old friends. "Hello, Tom!" he said. "Mind if I join you?"

"It's a free country," I said cooly. "How's the surf?"

"Unpredictable," he said. "I might win a few medallions though, if I'm lucky. You two wouldn't know anything about medallions, would you?"

"Not a thing," said Coxie blandly.

"I don't know you, do I?" I asked. He still looked a bit familiar.

"No. You *are* Tom Stratton, aren't you?" The wet-suit guy looked from me to Coxie and back.

"I'm Tom. This is Coxie."

"Hi, Coxie." He stuck out his hand, but Coxie didn't take it.

"Who are you?" asked Coxie. "What do you want?"

"Just to talk, Coxie." The guy held up his hands. "See? I'm not armed."

I relaxed a bit more. We were armed, or at least Coxie was.

"Why should you be armed?" asked Coxie. "Afraid of sharks in the mall?"

"Just joking." The wet-suit guy grinned. "Pretty neat trick, Tom, siccing the store detective on me. It took me some time to talk my way out of that one. By the way, my name's Baz. Tell me, have you ever met Lizba Smith?"

Both Coxie and I jumped when Baz mentioned Lizba's name, but we kept our faces straight. "Who?" I said.

Baz smiled. "Oh, you'd remember Lizba if you met her."

"Oh, yes!" said Coxie. "I remember Lizba. We met her ages ago, when we were little kids."

"Did she mention me?" Baz asked.

"I can't really remember," said Coxie bluntly. "I don't think so."

Baz looked at me. "Tom? Did Lizba say much to you?"

"Not that I remember." I tried to sound casual. "Like Coxie says, it was ages ago."

Baz shrugged. "Well, maybe she had other things on her mind."

She had. Like preventing a crime. Like living long enough to do what was necessary. Like protecting the past and the future from time travelers. Only it seemed as if she'd failed in that.

"How do you know Lizba?" I asked.

Baz laughed. "She's my mother."

That must be why he looked familiar, I thought. I was seeing a family resemblance. "What about Lizba?" I asked.

"She disappeared years ago," said Baz. "I'm anxious to find out what happened. Did she tell you her plans?"

I started to tell him she was dead, but Coxie hit me with his elbow. "She didn't say much," he said vaguely. "I've forgotten."

Baz smiled again. He seemed friendly, but Coxie obviously didn't like him much. "If you've forgotten, you can't help me," he said. "Too bad. I'm trying to find out what happened to Lizba, and to further her work. I thought we could have helped one another. My mistake."

He got up and shrugged. "So, you can't help me and you don't want my help, right?"

"Right," said Coxie. "Sorry."

Baz smiled ruefully and stuck out his hand. "No hard feelings?"

It seemed to me that Baz was the one who might have hard feelings. If I'd been trying to solve a mystery about *my* mother, I'd have wanted help. I felt bad about not telling him what we knew, but Coxie was right. We had to protect ourselves.

"I suppose not," said Coxie. He shook Baz's hand, then gathered up our sandwich wrappers and drink cartons and went to throw them in the trash.

I offered my hand. I tried not to let it tremble, but Baz noticed anyway. His smile faded. "Are you sure you don't want my help, Tom Stratton?" he said softly.

"What do you mean?"

"Well, that's a very bad case of nerve-burn you've got there."

"*What?*"

"Isn't that what's wrong with you, Tom?" asked Baz. "You seem to have all the classic symptoms of nerve-burn. Pretty far advanced case, too. I don't want to alarm you, but I don't think I've ever seen anyone so badly affected."

My legs gave way and I sat down again.

"Come on, Tom!" yelled Coxie. "We've got to go!"

"Wait a second, Coxie!" I called back. My heart was thumping with excitement, or maybe with dread. "Right," I said to Baz. "What's this nerve-burn? Can you cure it?"

"Trembling and progressive weakness," said Baz. "How old are you, Tom? Ten? Eleven?"

"Thirteen," I snapped.

"Then it's retarding your development, and it's worse than I thought. What treatment are you taking?"

"None," I said. "The doctors don't seem to know what's wrong."

"A roboscanner would pick it up immediately!"

"What's a roboscanner?"

Baz made a face. "Oh dear, I was forgetting. Never mind, Tom. This is the 20th century. You can't possibly have nerve-burn in the 20th century."

"Why not?"

"It's caused by exposure to a type of ray gun that won't be invented for many years to come. I'm sorry if I've upset you needlessly." He patted my shoulder and walked away.

"Wait!" I said.

Baz glanced back.

"Wait, Baz!"

People stared, and Coxie came over in a hurry. "Cut it out, Tom. Let him go!"

"I've got to talk to him."

"We agreed…" began Coxie.

"Look," I said. "It isn't you who has nerve-burn. It's serious, Coxie!"

While we were arguing, Baz interrupted. "Well?" he said.

"Does that ray gun look like…?" I was about to pull the sol-shot out of my pocket, but I realized I'd given it to Coxie. "Coxie?" I said. He shook his head, so I described the sol-shot instead. "Is it black, and about this big, with a safety catch and a lumpy barrel?"

"That certainly sounds like it. But where could you have seen one?"

"I was shot by one of those when we were in the ranges," I said. "More than a year ago. Could that have caused nerve-burn?"

"I'd say it's a certainty," said Baz.

"You mentioned a roboscanner," I prompted.

"I shouldn't have," said Baz. "Like the ray gun that caused the problem in the first place, roboscanners won't be invented for centuries."

"Then I'm stuck with this disease?"

"I'm afraid so," said Baz. "Of course, there's just a chance I could… But no, it isn't possible. If you boys could have helped me find Lizba, I might have been able to help you, but as it is, there's nothing I can do."

"That's blackmail!" said Coxie furiously.

"Nonsense!" said Baz. "I'd help Tom if I could, but without the medallions, I can't."

I glanced at Coxie. "We've got to help him," I said. I turned to Baz. "All right," I said. "What is it you want to know?"

Empty Pockets

"It's simple," said Baz, "I need to trace Lizba, and I need her time medallions."

"I'm sorry," I said, "but Lizba is dead. She was afraid people would use the technology for the wrong purposes. She destroyed the medallions and herself." I explained to Baz what Lizba had done.

"So she nobly sacrificed herself to save the world," said Baz. "That sounds like Lizba! But are you quite sure she died?"

I nodded. "Yes. We found her skull up in the Asbestos Ranges."

"How did you know it was hers?" asked Baz.

"She told us," I said.

"Where is this skull?"

"An old bat called Dr. Pennyfather is studying it. She lives just a little way past the mall."

"I must see it," said Baz. "I must be certain beyond a doubt that it is Lizba's."

"You'll never get it," I said. "Dr. Pennyfather won't show you – not unless you're another scientist. She wouldn't show *me,* and Coxie and I discovered it! She wouldn't listen, either."

Baz frowned, and I didn't blame him. I'd hate to think of someone studying my mom's skull. "I must get that skull," he said. "It would be worth... I mean, it would have great sentimental value to me. But I need the medallions before I'm able to help you, Tom."

"You must have some medallions yourself!" interrupted Coxie. "Otherwise, you couldn't have come here."

"I have a TDD – a Time-Displacement Device. TDDs can be used by only one person." Baz showed us a thing that looked like a wristwatch.

"You can't travel alone," said Coxie. "It kills you."

Coxie was certainly right about that. Lizba had died by traveling alone.

"Lizba's medallions were crude," said Baz. "The idea of being forced to travel in pairs is irresponsible. Using her system, travelers ran a risk of losing their partner. Then they'd be stranded, or forced to kidnap someone else!"

Coxie made a face. Palmer had kidnapped him for just that reason.

"How does this work?" I asked.

Baz hesitated. "When I redeveloped Lizba's original ideas, I applied the same basic principle, but improved on it. I can travel alone, and the TDD straps onto my wrist, so there's no risk of losing a medallion and being stranded."

"So why do you want the medallions?" asked Coxie. "You've advanced beyond them."

"Yes, but Lizba's prototypical TDDs would prove very interesting to temporal scientists such as myself. They would make a valuable addition to our heritage," said Baz. "I also want to help Tom! My TDD will translate only one person through time, so to take Tom to a time when his condition can be cured, I need the medallions."

"You could go home and make another gadget for Tom," Coxie pointed out.

"Yes," said Baz, "but it would take me a great deal of time. And time is something Tom can't afford. His condition could become critical at any…"

"I've got the medallions," I interrupted. "They're ruined, though." My insides felt as if I'd swallowed a lump of cold clay.

"Nevertheless," said Baz softly, "I'd like them back. Perhaps I could restore them."

"No," said Coxie loudly. "Lizba wanted the whole thing forgotten. We should respect that. Anyway, they're ruined, so you can't use them to help Tom."

I had an idea. "Why don't you use your TDD to go to the time when the original medallions were in good working order?"

Baz looked surprised and nervous. I wondered why. Surely that possibility was obvious!

"You could go back to when Coxie and I had them both," I added. Then I had an even better idea. "After I'm better, we could help Lizba deal with Palmer. Then she won't have to die!"

There was a short silence. Then Coxie turned to Baz. "Sure, why don't you? I would if it were my mom."

Baz looked exasperated. "It isn't so easy," he said. "For a start, I'd be doubling back in my own lifetime. If I met myself, or if someone who knew me then met my current self, it could cause a paradox. No, the only chance is if I could meet Lizba in a time outside our natural lifetimes. Unfortunately, I don't know where, or when, she went. I could be searching the centuries for the rest of my life!" He spread his hands. "Even if the medallions are ruined, I might be able to use them to focus on a particular time and place."

"We could go to the Asbestos Ranges when I'm well again," I said. "We can go back and save Lizba."

"How could we?" said Coxie roughly. "You and I were already there, Tom. We didn't see our current selves, and we didn't see Baz. It's impossible."

"We could have been hiding," I said, but I saw that Baz and Coxie were right. Undoing what had happened to Lizba would be very difficult.

"The medallions?" repeated Baz. "I must have them if I'm going to be any help to you."

"They're in my pocket," I said. Coxie began tugging my elbow. "Quit it, Coxie!"

"Your friend doesn't trust me," said Baz.

"Listen…" said Coxie.

"No, *you* listen, Coxie!" I said. "You didn't want to use them, remember? They're mine now, and I'm going to give them to Baz." I reached into my pocket.

First, I pulled out a feather.

"That must be Cracker's," said Coxie.

Then I pulled out a handkerchief covered with a wad of bubble gum. I felt in the other pocket, and pulled out fifty cents and a pencil. That was that. I'd run out of pockets. The time medallions were gone.

I felt really sick, the way you do when you sit down to do a test and you suddenly realize you're being tested on chapter five and you've only studied chapter four.

"The medallions?" said Baz again.

"I had them," I muttered. "They were in my pocket." I turned to Coxie. "You didn't take them, did you?"

"Of course not," said Coxie.

"They couldn't have fallen out," I said.

"You must have left them somewhere," said Coxie. "Did you leave them at my place?"

"No, I haven't had them out… Wait a minute! I was trying to show them to Dr. Pennyfather, but she wasn't interested. I thought I put them back in my pocket, but maybe I dropped them instead. I was in a hurry." My hands had been shaking a lot, too, but I wasn't going to say that.

"So the medallions are in the same place as the skull?" said Baz.

"Probably." I groaned. I couldn't think of a worse place for them, except maybe the middle of the sea.

"Let's go," said Baz.

A Warning

"We'll show you where Dr. Pennyfather lives," I offered, "but you'll have to do the talking. And get some different clothes first."

Baz touched the gadget on his wrist, and flickered out of sight. When we saw him again, he was wearing shorts and a bright shirt with the tag still hanging from the neck. "Better?"

Coxie and I stared. "You stole those from a store, didn't you?" said Coxie.

"They're not real clothes," said Baz. "It's just a holographic illusion built into the suit."

They looked real to me. "What about the tag?" I said, pointing.

"Is that wrong?" There was another flicker and the tag was gone.

"I wish I could do that," I said. "Just think, Coxie. You could wear cool grungy clothes to school and look as if you were in uniform."

"What's the use of wearing cool clothes if nobody can see them?" scoffed Coxie.

He had a point. I was still trying to come up with an answer when we reached the cul-de-sac where Dr. Pennyfather lived.

By now it was late afternoon, and the wall looked really forbidding. It looked like the sort of place a dragon might live behind – well, Dr. Pennyfather *was* a bit of a dragon. "You'll have to use that squawk-box," I told Baz. "She doesn't like me and she would probably recognize my voice."

Baz pressed the button on the intercom. "Dr. Pennyfather? I need to see you urgently."

After a short while, the gate opened, and Dr. Pennyfather peered through. Coxie and I crouched behind the open gate. "What do you want?" she asked Baz suspiciously.

Baz smiled. "Good day, I'm Dr. Smith. We need to discuss some important artifacts that may have come into your possession."

"Any artifacts in my possession have been come by legitimately, and I have no obligation to discuss them with anyone."

"Not these. They were left here inadvertently."

"That is not my problem."

Baz stuck his foot in the gate as she tried to close it. "Perhaps I should get to the point, Dr. Pennyfather. I believe Tom Stratton visited you today?"

"If you want to intervene for that tiresome little brat, you're simply wasting your breath, Dr. Smith," said Dr. Pennyfather. "Amateurs! Let them make one lucky discovery and they think they can get away with murder!"

"How true," said Baz. "I am not here to speak on his behalf, but on my own. This morning, Tom Stratton had some valuable antique medallions that belonged to my mother. I think he hoped they would impress you. Did he show them to you?"

"No," said Dr. Pennyfather.

"Then he must have disposed of them on your premises, for they were not in his possession when I apprehended him this afternoon."

"You'd better leave," said Dr. Pennyfather. "This has nothing to do with me."

"May I be allowed to make a quick search? I cannot believe a scientist such as yourself would allow unique anthropological artifacts to fall into the wrong hands."

Baz seemed to be blackening my character right and left! Then I peered around the gate and saw Dr. Pennyfather's eyes narrow. She had squinty little eyes at the best of times, and now they practically disappeared. "Unique anthropological artifacts?" she said.

"Exceedingly," said Baz. "Twelve centuries old, at least. It is imperative that I find them."

"Come on then," said Dr. Pennyfather. "But I warn you! I have surveillance cameras on the grounds."

"Excellent! We could study the film of Tom Stratton's visit and find out precisely what he did with the medallions." Still talking, Baz went through the gate.

"Now what?" asked Coxie.

"I guess we wait," I said.

We waited for ages. I began to feel cold and scared. I hate depending on other people, and since I'd been ill, I'd had to depend on a lot of people. Mom and Dad, my friends, the teachers at school, doctors, and so on. At first, I had depended on the doctors to make me well, but how could they help? How could they diagnose a disease that wouldn't exist for centuries?

Suddenly, I felt a bitter rush of disappointment in Lizba. She'd seen Palmer shoot me with the sol-shot. Why hadn't she warned me? I tried to think back. "Hey Coxie," I said. "Lizba never said anything at all about nerve-burn, did she?"

"Not that I remember," said Coxie. "I wasn't with you all the time though."

"She didn't," I said. "I know she didn't. Coxie, why didn't she warn me about what was going to happen?"

"Maybe she didn't want to scare you," said Coxie. "Maybe you were just unlucky. Perhaps people who get shot have one chance in a hundred of getting nerve-burn."

"Sure!" I said. "More likely she didn't care what happened as long as I finished the job."

"There wasn't anything she could have done," said Coxie, but he didn't sound sure.

"Anyway," I said. "Why did she make me destroy the computer if she'd already given her notes to Baz?"

"Weird," agreed Coxie. "She died so no one would have the medallion technology, but she'd already handed it over. *If* Baz is telling the truth."

"Maybe she didn't count Baz," I said. "After all, he *is* her son."

"So he says," said Coxie. He looked at his watch. "Did you know it's nearly four?"

That put me in a bind. Even if I hurried I'd probably miss the bus, and there was no way I wanted to leave town now. "Do you think your mom would mind if I stayed the night?" I asked.

Coxie gulped. "Well…"

"You don't have to sound so pleased," I said rather sarcastically. "You've stayed with *me* plenty of times."

"I'm going to the movies tonight," said Coxie.

"I can still stay at your place," I said. "I don't feel like going out, anyway."

"I guess we can ask," said Coxie. "Let's go."

"What about Baz?"

"Leave him a note," suggested Coxie.

I dug out a pencil, and Coxie handed me a crumpled piece of paper from his pocket. I smoothed it out and wrote a note to Baz. I added Coxie's telephone number and asked Baz to call as soon as he could. I stuck the note to the intercom with bubble gum.

"He won't know how to use a phone," said Coxie.

"If he can use TDDs, a phone won't give him much trouble," I said.

But Baz didn't telephone. He was waiting for us right outside Coxie's front gate.

"How did you get here so soon?" asked Coxie.

Baz flickered like a faulty lightbulb. "No time to talk," he said. He flickered again. "I've got the medallions, and I have to go…" He waved the medallions in front of me.

"What about my nerve-burn?" I yelled.

"I haven't forgotten, Tom. Listen, you might meet two other travelers. Don't believe anything they say about me. They're my enemies."

"What?"

"They're Palmer's friends." Baz flickered again, and this time he disappeared.

CHAPTER 11

A Policeman Calls

"Palmer's friends!" I groaned loudly "I don't like the sound of that."

"Maybe we should stay home tonight," Coxie said.

"That's no good," I said hollowly. "They can catch us anywhere."

"Wonder where Baz just went?" said Coxie.

"Wonder *when* he went, you mean," I muttered. You can't use time travel to move in space, you can only move in time. You can still disappear and appear in different places, though, by going forward or backward in time, moving to a new place, then returning to the present.

"That gadget of his is more accurate than the ones we had," said Coxie. "He turned up just as we got here."

"I hope Palmer's friends don't come here," I said. "I suppose they're after Baz because he's Lizba's son."

"I wish Baz didn't know where I live," grumbled Coxie, "and what if Mom saw him disappear?"

"She'll think her eyes are playing tricks on her." I wanted to get inside before I collapsed.

Coxie's mom hadn't seen Baz at all, but she *was* in a bit of a dither. "Boys! Where have you been? Tom missed his bus!"

"Sorry, Mom," said Coxie. "We went to Dr. Pennyfather's place because Tom left something there. Can he stay the night?"

"If it's all right with his parents," said Coxie's mom.

I called home. Mom seemed really pleased that I wanted to stay. "You're having a good time, then?" she said. "What did you find out?"

"I'll tell you when I get home, Mom." I crossed my fingers, hard, because before I saw Mom again I might be traveling through time. I might be cured! Then again, maybe I'd lost my chance. If Palmer's friends were after Baz, he might not have time to worry about my problems.

"I just hope Baz doesn't get caught," I said to Coxie while his mom was putting the Noise Machine to bed. "And I hope he's careful if he finds the medallions. If he takes them away before we used them, things might *un*happen."

"Maybe," said Coxie. He paused, then added, "Then again, if we'd never gone time traveling, if *that* unhappened, you wouldn't have been shot in the first place and you wouldn't have nerve-burn now."

I hadn't thought of that. Maybe Baz wouldn't need to take me into the future for a cure. Maybe he could arrange to have the nerve-burn unhappen instead.

"If he does, I won't be here," I said.

"I won't be here, either," said Coxie. "If it hadn't been for time traveling, I would have kept going to the Adventurers. If I hadn't quit, Wattsie wouldn't have come to see Mom about it, and they wouldn't have married. The Noise Machine wouldn't have been born and…" He groaned. "Gee, Tom, the things you get me into!"

"Maybe we could just undo what happened to me, and leave your life alone," I said.

"Baz will be doing the undoing, so he'll choose what he undoes," said Coxie. "There's something fishy about that guy, Tom. He's in too much of a hurry. If there's anything time travelers have plenty of, it's time. Why didn't he just go home and make you a TDD? He could have been back here in seconds. Or even less."

"Baz is all right," I said. "Don't forget, he has Palmer's gang after him."

"I hope he's all right, for your sake," said Coxie.

It's a horrible feeling, knowing you've got a disease from the future. It's also unpleasant to know you could suddenly lose nearly two years' worth of memories. Would we notice if it happened? Or would we blink and find ourselves somewhere else?

It made me dizzy, just thinking about everything that would be affected if Baz undid two years. I guess that's why I agreed to go to the movies with Coxie. His mom lent me the money for a ticket.

"I'll meet you outside the theater when the movie's over," she said.

"That's all right, Mom. We'll walk home," said Coxie. "It's only a few blocks."

"Tom? How do you feel about that?"

I felt awful, but I managed a weak grin. "I'm all right, Mrs. Watts."

We were just about to leave when there was a phone call from Mom.

"Tom, have you done anything you shouldn't have done?" she asked.

"No," I said. "Why?"

"I've just had a strange call from the police," said Mom. "It seems Dr. Pennyfather has lodged a complaint against you."

"Well! She was just as rude to me as I was to her! Even more!" I said.

"It's not about rudeness," said Mom. "That skull has been stolen, and Dr. Pennyfather is blaming you."

"I didn't steal it!" I said. "I didn't even see it! The old bat just yelled at me out in her yard, then practically threw me out."

"According to the police, she thinks you must have crept back later," said Mom.

"Well, I didn't."

"I didn't think you had." Mom sighed. "The police are coming to talk to you this evening. I'd better square it with Coxie's mom. If there's any real trouble, you let me know and Dad and I'll come right away."

I handed the phone to Coxie's mom.

"What was all that about?" asked Coxie.

"Lizba's skull's been stolen, and Dr. Pennyfather thinks I did it. The cops are coming here."

"Oh, great!" said Coxie. "Mom's going to love that!"

Coxie's mom wasn't too pleased, but I couldn't blame her. No one wants the cops on their doorstep. It's bad for the family reputation.

"I didn't do it," I told her. "It's all a mistake."

"Of course," she said, but she kept giving me these doubtful little looks. And when Sergeant Kerry arrived, he gave me the same looks, too.

"You seemed extremely interested in this skull, Tom," he said.

"I still am," I said. "But if I'd been planning a heist, would I have been asking you about it?"

"Probably not," said Sergeant Kerry.

"When did it happen?" I asked. "I've been with Coxie most of the day, so maybe I have an alibi."

"That's the trouble," said Sergeant Kerry. "Since the alarms and security system were bypassed, the theft could have taken place anytime during the past three days or nights. Dr. Pennyfather says she had no occasion to examine the skull until this evening. She went to verify a measurement, and found the skull had been removed from the storeroom."

"I'm sure Tom had nothing to do with it," said Coxie's mom. "He only arrived this morning and he's been with my son ever since."

Sergeant Kerry looked puzzled. "You haven't been on Dr. Pennyfather's premises, Tom?"

"Only this morning," I said. "I went to find out what she was going to do with the skull."

"Did you see it?"

"I didn't even go in the house. She threw me out."

"How long were you there?"

"I got there about nine, and left soon after," I said.

"Can anyone verify the fact that you left her house right away?"

"She can. And I went into a clothes store at the mall. I thought someone was following me, so I told the assistant. The store detective stopped the guy while I went out the back. They'd both remember me, I think."

Coxie's mom gawked at me. "Tom! I didn't know anything about this!" she said.

"It was just a mistake," I said. "It turned out the guy was someone who knew me. At least, I knew his mother."

"And you haven't been back to Dr. Pennyfather's premises today." Sergeant Kerry put away his notes. He obviously thought he was wasting his time.

"Coxie and I were outside her place at about 3:30," I said. "We saw her let a visitor in."

"I see." Sergeant Kerry put on his hat. "That would have been Dr. Smith. Dr. Pennyfather mentioned him."

"What happens now?" I asked.

"I'm sure you have nothing to worry about, Tom. Since a sophisticated alarm system was bypassed in the theft, it seems unlikely that anyone your age could have been involved."

I know kids my age who can make electronic circuits sit up and beg, but I didn't say so. "Thanks," I said instead.

"However," said Sergeant Kerry, "I'll give you some advice, Tom. Stay away from Dr. Pennyfather's place."

"The boys were just off to the movies," said Coxie's mom. "Is that all right?"

"That's fine," said Sergeant Kerry. "You're sure this person who followed you is on the level, Tom?"

"He's cool. Coxie and I were talking to him this afternoon," I said. "Can we go now? We don't want to miss the movie."

"I'd offer you a lift in the police car," said Sergeant Kerry, "but I'm not allowed to use it for innocent boys."

He laughed and left, and Coxie and I went to the movies. The movie had started, but we hadn't missed too much.

During a slow part of the movie, Coxie decided to get some popcorn. I stayed put in my seat. I was dog-tired, so I thought I was dreaming when I saw Dr. Pennyfather coming down the aisle.

Interview with
the Old Bat

She was peering around and arguing loudly with one of the ushers. Oh no, I thought. The old bat's looking for me!

No normal anthropologist chases kids into movie theaters, but then Dr. Pennyfather was no normal anthropologist. I thought about making a break for it, but that would make her think I was guilty. I scrunched down, but she came along the row and sat down beside me.

"That's my friend's seat," I said.

"Then let's discuss this in the lobby," she replied.

I didn't want to discuss it at all, but I followed her out. I looked around for Coxie, but he'd disappeared.

"What do you want?" I said. "I didn't take the skull, so there's no use hassling me."

Dr. Pennyfather snorted. "This isn't about the skull; it's about the medallions."

"What medallions?"

"Don't pretend to be stupid, young man. When you forced your way onto my premises this morning…"

"You let me in!" I said furiously.

"You had some metallic artifacts," she said, "that you very carelessly left on my lawn."

"I meant to put them back in my pocket."

"Tell me about them. Every detail."

"You weren't interested this morning," I said coldly. "You told me to get out."

"Listen, young man…"

"Stop calling me that," I said. "My name is Tom Stratton. And why should I help you? You threw me out, and you sicced the police on me. Now you're following me around. I didn't take the skull, and the medallions have nothing to do with you."

"If they are clues to the history of the skull, they have very much to do with me," said Dr. Pennyfather. "And you obviously know something about them. Tell me."

"No," I said. "You wouldn't listen before. You wouldn't believe me anyway. What was it you said this morning? That the only interest you had in *me* was in my absence? Well, I'm saying the same to you. If you want to see the movie, go and watch it. If you don't, go home."

Dr. Pennyfather's face was turning red. She could dish it out, but she obviously couldn't take it! I saw her take a deep breath, and I knew she really wanted this information. "All right, Tom," she said. "I'm going to do you the favor of treating you like a fellow rational adult."

"Gee, *thanks*," I growled. I didn't think that was much of an honor. If Dr. Pennyfather was a rational adult, I was King Kong.

"Tell me about Dr. Smith."

"I don't know any Dr. Smith."

"Of course you do," she said impatiently. "You left this for him."

She held out the note I'd left, and I could have kicked myself. Imagine being stupid enough to sign my name and give Coxie's phone number. I'd never thought that *she* would get ahold of it.

"You mean Baz," I said. "I don't know him well. I knew his mother."

"And his mother is the person who originally owned the medallions?"

"Right. They were damaged, and she left them with me about a year ago. I was going to show them to you, but you couldn't be bothered. Then Baz wanted them back. I told him I thought I'd dropped them at your place, so he went to get them."

Dr. Pennyfather was staring at me.

"It's true," I said tiredly. My hands were beginning to shake again.

"Very well. Where and when did you first meet Ms. Smith?"

"Who the heck is Ms. Smith?"

"Dr. Smith's mother," said Dr. Pennyfather.

"Oh. I met her a year or so ago up in the Asbestos Ranges, and she gave me the medallions the same day." (It wasn't the same day, of course. The days were hundreds of years apart, but there was no use telling Dr. Pennyfather that.)

"Where and when did she first obtain them?" The old bat could teach Sergeant Kerry a thing or two about grilling suspects.

"She made them."

As soon as I'd said it, I knew I'd made a mistake. Dr. Pennyfather knew, too. "How very odd," she said triumphantly. "Dr. Smith believes the artifacts are several centuries old. His mother must have been an extremely venerable lady, or an untruthful one."

I shrugged. "That's what she told me," I said. "You're the expert. What do *you* think?"

"I think you know far more than you're telling me, Tom Stratton."

"Why didn't you examine them when you had them?" I asked.

She frowned. "Dr. Smith left rather suddenly," she said, and for the first time she sounded a bit uncertain.

Wow! Baz must have flicked back (or forward) in time and practically vanished right in front of her. No wonder she was interested! No wonder she'd bothered to chase after me!

"Have you known Dr. Smith for long?"

"I never met the guy before today, all right? His mom left the medallions with me. He wanted them back. I told him I must have dropped them at your place this morning. I didn't want to tangle with you again, so I sent him to get them himself. He obviously did. End of story."

"You don't have his home address? Or a contact number where I can reach him?"

"I want to see the movie," I said, trying not to sway. "Good-bye, Doctor."

Dr. Pennyfather dug in her pocket for a notebook and pencil and scribbled down some numbers. She ripped out the page and held it out to me. "If Dr. Smith contacts you, or if you remember anything more about him, telephone me at this number," she said. "It's very important."

I considered tearing up the telephone number and scattering it around the lobby, but that would have been littering, so I just shoved it in my pocket and went back into the theater. I didn't look back.

The movie was good, I suppose, but I couldn't really concentrate. I was much too busy thinking. No wonder Dr. Pennyfather was interested, if Baz had disappeared right in front of her! I wondered what she really thought about the medallions. They were melted, and I didn't think she could have guessed they were from the future. Anyway, Baz had them now. And Baz had gone off with them, somewhere in time, evading Palmer's friends. Baz was trying to find the medallions in working condition. He could be anywhere in any year. He might decide to never come back at all.

I shivered. If Baz didn't come back, I didn't have much hope for my chances.

I'd really overdone it that day, and when the movie ended, I was exhausted. The thought of walking back to Coxie's place made me wilt, but I couldn't bring myself to call his mom and ask for a ride. I'd already caused her enough trouble.

I hoped some of Coxie's friends might offer to give us a ride back. I could pretend I had twisted my ankle or something. "See anyone you know, Coxie?" I asked.

"No," said Coxie. "What happened to you during the movie?"

"I was getting grilled by the old bat," I said. "Dr. Pennyfather thinks there's something very weird about Baz."

"Well, there *is*," said Coxie. "Wait a minute! Do you mean she came in *here?*"

"Yes. She was asking a bunch of questions about Baz and the medallions."

We were walking slowly, and just about everyone else had gone. The next thing I knew, two people appeared from behind us. They split up so they were walking on either side of us. "Tom Stratton?" said the man.

"What?" I stopped and looked sideways.

"Are you Tom Stratton?"

"Yes. Hey! Get your hands off me!" The man had taken a firm hold of my elbow, and I could see Coxie was being held in an armlock by the woman.

"Be quiet," said the man. "We need to talk to you."

"If you don't let me go, I'll scream," I said.

"Calm down," said the woman. "We won't hurt you."

"Let go!" said Coxie.

"You're coming with us," said the man. He sounded so much like a cop in a bad thriller that I almost laughed.

"Why should we?" I asked.

"Because you must. You have become involved in a situation that should never have happened. You may have information that can be of great assistance to us. You must return the sol-shot, and also the time medallions."

"You've been watching too much television," I said. I was shaking, but I tried to sound bored. "Coxie and I don't know what you're talking about."

The man glanced at his partner, and they both reached for their belts.

"Stop!" said Coxie.

Somehow, he'd pulled the sol-shot out of his pocket, and he was pointing it at the woman. She let him go and backed away. I didn't blame her. I'd seen what a sol-shot could do.

"Let Tom go," said Coxie. His voice was shaking, but he wasn't running out on me.

The man let go of my arm. "You really must come with us," he said. "It's for your own good."

"*Must* nothing!" said Coxie. "If you're Palmer's friends, we don't have to do anything for you. You've got no right messing up our lives! Come on, Tom."

We backed away. Coxie kept the sol-shot in his hand. I knew the safety catch was still on, but they didn't.

Coxie ducked around a corner, and dragged me after him. "Let's go to the mall," hissed Coxie, "and take a shortcut home."

We heard footsteps coming, then suddenly they stopped. I glanced back just in time to see the man and woman vanish.

The Choice

"They've gone," I said, and flopped down, breathing hard.

"But where," said Coxie. "And *when?*"

We soon found out, because the pair popped into view ahead of us. While they were getting their bearings, we ducked behind the fountain where we had met Baz earlier that day.

It's creepy being chased by time travelers. They can pop in and out, and appear where you least expect them. You're not safe from them anywhere. We couldn't even go to Coxie's house and lock ourselves in. A time traveler only had to come to Coxie's front door, go back a few hundred years, take four or five steps forward, come back to the present, and be inside the house.

I think the chase lasted about twenty minutes; it seemed like two days. I guess they would have caught us eventually, but then Coxie backed right into Baz, who'd appeared behind us. I think Baz was as surprised as we were, because he was tapping the TDD on his wrist when I looked around. He soon figured out what was happening, though. "Looks like you boys need some help," he said. Baz snaked his arm around Coxie and took the sol-shot. "My, where did you get *this?*" he asked, turning it over, but keeping his eye on the other time travelers.

"It was Lizba's," I gasped.

"What luck!" said Baz cheerfully. "Sit down, Tom, while I send this pair on their way."

I sat down.

"Really, James," said Baz to the other man. "I thought you would have more sense. Were you trying to abduct these two lads? That hardly fits in with your high ideals."

The man called James ignored him. "It is imperative that you come with us, Tom," he said. He still sounded like a bad actor pretending to be a cop. "Don't trust this man. He's a wanted criminal, and he's meddling with things he doesn't understand. Besides that, you are in a very serious situation. You have an illness that…"

"I've got nerve-burn," I said. "I know. You didn't have to grab me to tell me that."

"We can offer treatment, if you agree to our terms," said the woman.

"Sure. So can Baz. And there are no terms with Baz. I helped him; he'll help me."

James turned to the woman. "I told you, Maria. We should have stunned them first."

"We had to verify their identity," she said.

"How many cases of nerve-burn could there be in the 20th century?"

She shrugged. "We couldn't even really be certain it *was* nerve-burn."

"It seems certain now," said James. "Look how pale he is. We're just in time."

"If I *do* have it, it's Palmer's fault!" I snapped. "He shot me."

"Palmer?" said Maria quickly. "Palmer shot you?"

"Well, I didn't give the nerve-burn to myself."

"A blast of active power wouldn't cause any real lasting damage," said Maria. "We had assumed long-term exposure to an exhausted…"

"Well, this *has* been a lovely chat," interrupted Baz. "Tom, I've traced the working medallions. Are you ready to go get them?"

I looked at Baz and then at James and Maria. "What about Coxie?" I asked.

"We don't need Coxie," said Baz. "Come on. I can have you back in a second or two."

I didn't really want to go on my own with Baz. "Come on, Coxie," I said.

"No, *you* come on," said Coxie. "Let's go home and let them sort themselves out. They're all after something."

"No, Tom, please come over here," said Maria. "You must trust us."

"Sure," said Baz. "He's really going to trust a couple of kidnappers whose friend shot him."

"That's ridiculous," said Maria. "Tom, this man is nothing but trouble. He's a thief and a…"

"Tom, have I ever tried to make you do anything you didn't want to do?" asked Baz.

I'd had enough. They were arguing over me as if I were a piece of meat. "I wish you'd all leave us alone," I said. "We don't owe any of you anything. If you won't help me, go away."

There was a little silence after that, and then we heard the tapping of heels. I looked around and there was the old bat herself, Dr. Pennyfather. I think I groaned.

"Dr. Smith," said Dr. Pennyfather, "I have very good reason to believe you have not been completely honest with me. I must insist that you explain how it was that you were able…"

"Yes, you explain it to her," I said to Baz. "I'm going."

I turned away, but Baz put his hand on my shoulder, and Coxie and the others disappeared.

It wasn't like time traveling with the medallions. I felt as if I'd left my stomach behind, and everything looked wrong. We were still in the mall, and it was still dark, but it just all somehow felt wrong. The mall seemed to flicker, then steadied.

I let out a yell, and then I doubled over. I felt really sick. "What's going on, Baz?" I croaked. "I said I didn't want to come."

"Never mind that now," said Baz. "We've got to get to Dr. Pennyfather's place."

There was another flicker, and he tapped the TDD.

"Why?" I said. "If you wanted to see her, there she just was. And you've already got the medallions."

Baz laughed. "I also have the sol-shot." He tossed up the ray gun and caught it. "Now all I need is the skull and I've got all the proof I need of Lizba's fate."

"The skull's been stolen," I muttered. "Remember? And I bet you did it."

"Not yet," said Baz. "I haven't stolen it yet."

"Someone has. Sergeant Kerry and Dr. Pennyfather said so."

"They're not important. Come on, Tom." He grabbed my arm and pulled me upright.

"Leave me alone," I said. "I want to rest."

"You can rest all you want in a month or so," said Baz cheerfully. "It's lucky I found you in time. Another few weeks and I'd have been too late." He laughed again. "That is, I would have had to go away and come back earlier."

He hurried me through the mall. At one point my legs gave way, but that didn't stop Baz. He just bent down and threw me across his shoulders. After a short while, we were outside Dr. Pennyfather's place.

"Right," said Baz, putting me down. "Let's get that skull. I need to verify its identity."

"It's not there," I said. "I told you."

"Tom, Tom, you are so very literal! Now listen. This is two nights ago from your perspective. Dr. Pennyfather is currently enjoying a dinner out with a Dr. Kane."

"You're crazy!" I said. "Those alarms will go off the second you try to get in, and you'll have the cops on us!"

Baz thought that was very funny. "No, Tom."

"The security cameras will pick us up."

"No they won't."

"Those other people will catch you."

"Not while I have you as a hostage. How many paces do you think it would take to reach the house from here?"

"I don't know and I don't care." I wanted to get away from Baz, but I couldn't run, and besides, he'd brought me back in time. Only a couple of days back, but I couldn't stay here. I'd be in two places at once.

"You'd *better* care," said Baz.

"Why?"

"If we get it wrong you might find yourself suddenly materializing inside a wall."

A Theft in Time

"Fortunately, I don't leave these things to chance," said Baz when he thought I'd suffered enough. "We will need thirteen paces to the house and three more to clear the interior walls."

There was another flicker and my stomach dropped again. I struggled not to be sick.

"What's *wrong* with that thing?" I gasped.

"I don't know," said Baz. "It doesn't seem to work the way it should."

"You ought to know. You said you made it."

"I lied," said Baz smugly.

We were standing among trees. "Sixteen paces," said Baz. "Will you walk, or do I carry you?"

"You can carry me," I said sourly. "Then I won't end up in any walls. You're a creep, Baz. You don't care about me at all. Not like Lizba did."

"Did Lizba care about you when she let you get shot?" He still sounded amused.

I didn't want to think about that at the moment. "*When* are we now?"

"About A.D. 1700, give or take a decade." Baz paced out the distance, there was another flicker, and we were standing in a dimly lit hallway. My stomach couldn't take much more of this. Neither could I.

"Here we are," said Baz, "right back where we were." He laughed.

There were some really ugly wooden masks on the walls, but I didn't have time to stare. Baz dragged me along the hallway and made me open a door. "In here, I think," he said.

It was a storage room full of jars, boxes, and crates. "Open the boxes," said Baz. He had the sol-shot in his hand, and now he wasn't smiling anymore. I did as he said. It was very hard work; my hands were numb and almost useless.

"Why do you need me?" I asked.

"You're a hostage to keep James and Maria away," said Baz. "I also need you to help identify the skull."

The boxes were full of bones, pieces of china, and so on. It would have been interesting if I hadn't been sick and terrified. By now I'd realized that Baz was going to make me steal the skull for him. After that, he'd just disappear and leave me to make it as best I could.

Lizba's skull was in the fourth box I opened. I stood looking down at it for a moment, then I went on to open another box. "Have you found it?" asked Baz.

I lifted out a skull from the box I'd just opened. It was brownish and broken. "This could be it."

Baz took it and looked at it closely. Then he smiled at me. "This is the skull of the selfless Lizba Smith?"

"It might be."

Baz put the skull back in the box. "Nice try, Tom. Now find the right one. Don't bother trying to fool me again. I have the measurements from Lizba Smith's file."

"She wasn't your mother, was she?" I said. I opened another box. I was playing for time, but I don't know why I bothered.

"What makes you think that?" said Baz.

"You don't care about her at all. And now I think I remember where I've seen you before."

"Really?" He didn't seem too worried.

"You were in Lizba's lab when I wrecked the computer. You were one of Palmer's gang, weren't you?"

He didn't answer.

"So that means James and Maria are on the other side. I should have gone with them. Who are they, anyway? Friends of Lizba's?"

Baz grinned. "They never met Lizba Smith. They're meddlers from the future. *My* future. Oh, they have very high-sounding ideals about clearing up anomalies in the past, but when you come down to it, they're no better than me. If they think time travel is so bad, what are they doing with these?" And he waved his TDD at me.

"Why do you really want the skull?" I asked. "And why did you really want the medallions? You're not still trying to kill Kane?"

"I never cared all that much about Kane," said Baz. "I need the skull to prove that Lizba Smith is dead. Since there were no reliable witnesses, and Lizba was as sly as they come, I suspected she had simply moved forward in time. That meant she could turn up any year, or could even be behind the activities of the wonderful James and Maria. I *know* Palmer is dead, but the whereabouts of Lizba have always been a mystery. Without proof she's dead, I can't be sure she won't pop up to bother me again.

"In a way, I was hoping she might be alive. It would have been interesting to talk with her, and with you as a hostage, I could very well have persuaded her to give me the medallions."

"You already have time travel," I said. "You said you developed it from Lizba's notes! You could go to her in her past if you're that keen."

"I tried to develop time travel from an early version of *Palmer's* notes," corrected Baz. "But, they're incomplete, and I haven't been very successful."

"What about *that?*" I pointed to the TDD on his arm. "That seems to work."

"This isn't mine," said Baz. "I took it away from James. A pretty neat trick, don't you think? James comes zipping back through the years, trying to stop my little experiments, and I knocked him out with a sol-shot and removed his TDD. The only problem is, these things aren't very reliable, particularly when they're used to translate two people at once. They really *are* designed for solo use, and this one could go wrong at any time. In fact, it's flicked me back to my own time quite often." He smiled again. "Nice thought, isn't it, Tom? Every translation could be my last and I'd be stuck at home. Or maybe here in the 20th century. That really would be an anomaly. Now, get that skull and then tell me exactly when and where I can find the medallions in good working order."

Baz was getting impatient, so I went back and picked up Lizba's skull. I'd forgotten how beautiful it was, a pearly blue-green color. "This is it," I said.

Baz took it casually. "Yes, so it is. I recognize the contours. Then Lizba Smith really is dead." He shook his head. "She probably wouldn't have helped me anyway."

Baz made me replace the boxes, then we left. There was another flicker. I felt… well, I felt like dying.

"Where… I mean, *when* are we now?" I asked wearily.

"This is the same time we left the mall. Now for the medallions," reminded Baz. "Where and when can I easily obtain them, Tom?"

I groaned. "I can't think," I said. "It's ages ago."

"You'd better think, for your own sake," said Baz. He sounded calm, but I could imagine what he might do if I didn't help. On the other hand, I couldn't let him take the medallions out of my past. He might undo Coxie's life and mess up mine even more. Besides, would *you* let a character like Baz loose with time medallions?

So, while I pretended to think about how Baz could get the medallions, I actually thought about how to stop him.

First, I considered sending Baz to the Asbestos Ranges, to the day before Coxie and I found the skull. His chances of locating the medallions there were pretty low. Then I realized he'd take me with him, and I didn't feel well enough to climb hills.

Next, I tried to remember where they really *had* been. Mostly in my bedroom at home. And at one time, Coxie and I had each had one. Coxie had never liked the medallions much. He'd wanted them both at one time, but only to keep me from using them…

"I've remembered," I said.

"Where and when?" said Baz.

"Coxie had the medallions in his dresser about a year and a half ago. If you pick the first Wednesday in May, at about noon, there'll be no one home."

"You wouldn't lie to me, Tom?"

"Listen," I said. "I don't care what happens in your time. Why should I? Should I fetch the medallions myself? I know where he kept them." I hoped Baz wouldn't want to chance me using them, and I was right.

"Good-bye, Tom," he said.

"Wait!" I said. "What about my nerve-burn? Are you coming back?"

"I doubt it," said Baz. "I'd cure you if I could, but that's impossible."

"But in your time..." I began.

"There's no cure in my time either," said Baz. "Your best chance is to go back to James and Maria, if they're still at the mall. They're from my future; maybe they can help."

"Thanks a lot," I said bitterly, but I was talking to the empty air.

Nerve-Burn

"Great," I muttered. "Just great."

I had sent Baz off on a wild-goose chase, because Coxie had never had the time medallions at his place in Devonport. Eighteen months ago he'd lived near me. I wondered what would happen. Baz would go to the place where Coxie lived now. Either there would be no one at home and Baz would search for nothing, or else there *would* be someone home. If so, I hoped they would call the cops. The police would never catch Baz, but they might hold him up for awhile and give me a chance to find the others. But who was I fooling? Baz could spend a year in the past and still pop up right now in my present. And he wouldn't be a happy time traveler when he did.

All I had was the time it would take him to walk to Coxie's house and back again, so I knew I'd better get to the mall. I just hoped James and Maria would still be there. I forced myself to walk. One foot in front of the other, one, two, one, two. As I started along the sidewalk, I hoped James and Maria had gotten rid of Dr. Pennyfather. I didn't think I could face more of her questions, particularly if she started going on about the skull. There was another thing: my fingerprints would be all over her storeroom now!

I wondered how I'd explain that to Sergeant Kerry and Mom and Dad, then I started getting a funny feeling that I'd never have to explain anything to any of them. All of a sudden, I couldn't feel my feet.

I looked down to see what was going on, but that was a mistake. The ground seemed to be heaving under me. I jerked upright and forced myself to keep going.

I made it halfway to the mall before I collapsed. One minute I was staggering along the sidewalk, the next I saw the cement coming toward me and I was flat on my face. When I tried to get up, I realized I couldn't move.

It wasn't like the time Palmer had shot me. Then, I'd been paralyzed. This time, I wasn't numb and I wasn't paralyzed. I could feel every bump and bruise, and they all hurt a lot. I remember pawing at the sidewalk, trying to push myself upright, and wondering vaguely why nothing was happening. That was when I realized I simply didn't have the strength to get up.

I think that's when it really hit me that I was going to die right there. I'd been trying to get to Maria and James, counting on a cure, but now it was too late. I could feel my life draining away, and I was shocked because it had all been so sudden. Back in the mall, I'd been feeling bad, but not all that much worse than I'd felt for months. Now I felt about fifty times worse. It must have been all that zipping around in time.

I tried to tell myself Coxie and James and Maria would find me soon, but I didn't really believe it. They didn't know where I was, and they didn't know when I was. For all they knew, Baz could have whisked me off to another century.

That's when I heard running footsteps. I couldn't see who it was, but somehow I knew it was Coxie and that he'd seen me. "Are you all right, Tom?" he said.

I think I made a sort of gurgle.

"It's all right, they've gone," said Coxie. "I managed to persuade them that they didn't need us after all." He laughed. "I figure Dr. Pennyfather had a bit to do with that! She wanted their names and addresses and everything. I think they were glad to get away from her. Of course, they had to walk around the corner before they left. It's bad enough that she saw Baz zip out. If she'd seen James and Maria do it, too, she'd have flipped her lid."

"How did you find me?" I muttered.

"I figured that Baz would go back a couple of days and steal the skull, so that meant you had to be near Dr. Pennyfather's place. Was I right, or was I right?" Coxie sounded very pleased with himself.

"He's got the sol-shot and he's gone looking for the medallions," I mumbled.

"Good riddance," said Coxie. "James and Maria will catch up with him before he does anything else. They don't approve of people from the future coming back here."

"*They* came back."

"That was only to catch Baz and to clear up a few anomalies. It's over now, for us, so get up. Mom'll be wondering what's taking us so long."

"I can't get up, Coxie," I said. "I've got nerve-burn, remember? And now you've sent James and Maria away, so I'm going to die. You didn't think of that, did you?"

There was silence. I could only see Coxie's feet and ankles, but I could imagine the look on his face. He might be bigger and stronger now, but he was still the same old Coxie, and I knew I'd hurt his feelings. "I thought you wanted them to go," he said finally.

"I'm going to die," I said again.

Coxie squatted and put his hand on my shoulder. "You can't get nerve-burn from being shot by one of those guns," he said. "Maria said the effect is only temporary."

"But Baz said... Oh, forget it." I knew I couldn't depend on anything Baz had said. "Fine," I muttered. "So how long is this temporary effect going to last?" My voice was slurring.

My hands and feet were numb now, and the backs of my legs were cold. I couldn't feel my face anymore, and soon I couldn't speak. I could hear Coxie saying something, and I thought how weird it was that I couldn't quite follow what he was saying.

Then I thought how weird it was altogether that Tom Stratton, who'd been time traveling through the centuries, should die right here and right now. If it had to happen at all, I'd rather die at home, or get killed fighting dinosaurs or monsters. Or maybe I'd rather die like Lizba, fighting for something I believed in. Only Lizba's death hadn't really achieved anything, had it? Time travel still existed, and now that Baz knew for certain she was dead, who knew what he would do. Then I thought it wouldn't make any difference to me. Nothing would make any difference to me now.

What made it all even worse was when Dr. Pennyfather came tapping up beside us. "What does he think he's doing?" Dr. Pennyfather asked Coxie loudly. "What's wrong with him?"

Timedetectors

Dr. Pennyfather sounded pretty mad, and it felt like she actually poked me with her toe. What sort of person pokes a dying kid with her toe? A Dr. Pennyfather sort of person. But then, maybe Dr. Pennyfather didn't really mean to be an old bat. She was just so interested in studying historical humans, that she had lost touch with how to deal with the living ones.

Another thing about Dr. Pennyfather: she was *not* stupid. And she had the courage of her convictions. She'd seen Baz and me disappear, and she'd seen Maria and James and Lizba's skull. She knew none of those things fit in with normal life in the 20th century, and she wanted to know more. Any normal person would have decided she was seeing things and gone to an eye doctor or a shrink. Not Dr. Pennyfather. She knew she was right.

Dr. Pennyfather prodded me again and demanded that I sit up and answer questions. "What happened to you?" she said. "Where is Dr. Smith?"

When I didn't answer, she crouched down. "Is he hurt?" she asked Coxie. "Did you see him fall?"

"He was like this when I got here," said Coxie.

"He seems to have had some sort of seizure," Dr. Pennyfather muttered. I don't think she was worried about me. She just wanted to question me about Baz.

"He hasn't been very well," said Coxie. "I think we should get him home."

Dr. Pennyfather rolled me over and poked my neck. "That's odd," she said. "There seems to be some sort of muscle spasm. Tom, what happened? Do you have any allergies? Did you hurt yourself?"

I gasped. By this point I was having serious trouble breathing.

"I suppose I should call an ambulance," Dr. Pennyfather sighed, pulling out her mobile phone. I don't know what she said, but there wasn't much of a wait before the ambulance came blazing up the street.

I remember seeing the red light and hearing the noise, then suddenly people were grabbing me and Dr. Pennyfather was explaining and Coxie was looking increasingly worried. Then I stopped breathing.

It's hard to describe what happened next. Have you ever listened to a radio that isn't tuned properly? Sometimes you hear two people talking at once, and the voices overlap. It was like that. I heard someone in the ambulance say: "We're losing him," and at the same time, I heard someone else say: "We've got him."

Then the lights went out. When they came back on, I was lying in a sort of tent, and there was red light all around me. Something very cold hit my neck, and I passed out again.

The next time I woke up, the red light had gone. So had the tent. I was still in bed, but this time I was covered with a sheet and I felt normal. I sat up and found my muscles had come back to life. *That* was a real relief, so I flopped back down and thought about it.

I'm in the hospital, I decided. Then I wondered where Mom and Dad were. And where was Coxie? I heard footsteps and I started to calm down. I even closed my eyes.

"You're awake." That's what people always say on television when someone's in the hospital, so of course I said, "No, I'm still asleep." I wasn't trying to be funny, it was just a reflex.

"You *are* awake," said the voice, and I groaned. It was Dr. Pennyfather.

"Look," I said, "I've had a horrible experience, and I don't want another one just yet. I want Mom and Dad. Where are they?"

Dr. Pennyfather loomed over me, so I sat up again.

"Never mind them," she said. "They're not here, and this is more important. How are you feeling?"

I gaped at her. I never thought Dr. Pennyfather would care about my health. Then I found out she *didn't* care. All she wanted was to find out what it felt like to be irradiated with red rays. She had a notebook and pencil, and she started grilling me.

"What do you remember? Did the red rays feel hot? Is your skin tender? Abnormally sensitive? Numb?"

"Look," I said finally, "are you a doctor? A doctor of medicine, I mean?"

"I am an anthropologist."

"But are you a doctor of medicine?"

"No."

"In that case, my health has nothing to do with you, and you can put that notebook away," I said. Then I remembered that she'd called the ambulance. "It's not that I'm ungrateful," I added.

Dr. Pennyfather's eyes gleamed. "Then you can demonstrate your gratitude by answering my questions."

She had a point, so I answered what I could, then she started poking around the equipment. That made me a bit nervous, because some of the equipment was connected to the bed – and *me*.

"Look, I wish you'd stop that," I said. She was still nosing around when Coxie came in, followed by James and Maria.

Call me stupid if you want, but it wasn't until then that I realized I wasn't in the local hospital. Well, how was I to know I'd been hauled into the future? Hospitals look and smell the same in the 35th century as they do in the 20th century.

Coxie sat down by the bed. "That was close," he said. "Listen, the timedetectors want to talk to us. Do you feel up to it?"

"Timedetectors?"

"James and Maria. They're cops from the Kane Foundation. Temporal investigators is what they call themselves. I call them timedetectors."

"The Kane Foundation? What's that?"

"Remember that guy Kane that Lizba thought was so important?" said Coxie. "The one that Palmer wanted to kidnap and maybe kill before he grew up? Well, Kane survived, and after Palmer's gang was disbanded, he thought everything was all right. Then one of them started messing around with time travel again."

"That'd be Baz," I said.

"Yes. He wasn't too successful, and there was really nothing anyone could pin on him, but Kane knew there might be trouble later. He started the Kane Foundation to develop time travel properly, then he had the technology locked away. He set up a task force to sort through history and find anomalies that indicated time travelers had been interfering when and where they shouldn't. It's James and Maria's job to go back and make things right."

"How? By grabbing people like us?" I said.

"Hey, don't knock it!" said Coxie. "If they hadn't made the grab, you'd be history."

Anomaly

"I *am* history if we're in the future," I said. "And so are you. What year is this?"

Coxie shrugged. "We're some time in the 35th or 36th century, I think. They won't tell us any more than that." He bent down. "That really tees off Dr. Pennyfather!"

"I bet," I said. "What's she doing here, anyway?"

Coxie winked at me. "James calls her an 'unavoidable complication.' I like James."

"Hmm," I said. I didn't feel like liking anyone just then, not even Coxie.

"So," I said to James. "I can see why you wanted to get Baz if he stole your TDD, but what do Coxie and I have to do with it?"

James glanced irritably at Dr. Pennyfather. "I think you should leave."

"I am not going anywhere," said Dr. Pennyfather. "You have kept me confined in this building for a week without answers, and now I demand my rights."

"Oh, let her stay, James," said Maria wearily. "It won't make any difference. Tom is the important one right now. And the major problem." She looked at me, and there was something in her eyes that worried me. The vet had a look like that when our old dog broke his leg.

"If I'm a problem, it's Palmer's fault, not mine," I said. "What's wrong with me?"

"Nothing," said Maria. She smiled. It was the first time I'd seen her look anything but bothered or bored, and I saw Coxie give her an admiring sideways look.

"What do you mean, nothing wrong with me?" I said. "I almost died back there! Maybe I *did* die back there! You don't die from nothing."

"Believe me, Tom," said Maria, "there is nothing wrong with you now. As a matter of fact, you don't need these anymore." She detached the tubes from my arms. You did have an extremely advanced case of nerve-burn, but your nerves and muscles seem to have satisfactorily regen…"

"Erhm!" said James. "He doesn't need to know that. Neither does *she*." (No prizes for knowing who he meant!)

Maria smiled again. "James is right. All you need to know is that the nerve-burn has been cured."

"How do you know? You said I couldn't have gotten it from being shot," I reminded.

"The treatment," interrupted Dr. Pennyfather. "I demand to know the treatment for this condition. The red spectra in the tent seemed to indicate the presence of some kind of radiation. Is that correct?"

James gave her a dirty look, but otherwise ignored her.

"The damage wasn't done by the original burst from the sol-shot," said Maria seriously. "Nerve-burn occurs from long-term exposure to a sol-shot with an exhausted solar pack. It was designed to recharge itself from solar radiation. Do you understand?"

I nodded. "We have solar panels and solar calculators."

"If deprived of solar radiation," continued Maria, "a sol-shot will feed off any available source of power – in this case, you!"

"Ugh!" said Coxie. "Like a vampire!"

"You might say that," said Maria. "It was designed as an emergency measure, but occasionally it backfires."

"That is preposterous!" said Dr. Pennyfather.

"Long-term exposure…" I said. "I kept the thing in a box under my bed. Would that have caused the problem?"

"It certainly would," said Maria.

"So it was my fault…" That meant it hadn't been Lizba's fault after all! It would never have occurred to her that I'd keep the thing under my bed! "I'd have gotten better then, once the sol-shot was recharged by the sun?" I said.

"No," said Maria. "The damage was far too advanced. You died. In fact, it was the report on your death that alerted us to the anomaly."

"What do you mean, my death? I'm alive, aren't I?"

"During our research, we discovered an account of the death of a child from a mystery condition. It seemed quite likely that it was nerve-burn," said Maria. "That fact pointed to temporal anomaly, because the first reported case of nerve-burn didn't occur until 3151, shortly after the sol-shot was developed. We decided to investigate, and during our research into your death, we found a few other anomalies: the presence of a skull from the 32d century and the report of a theft that seemed to point to the presence of a time traveler."

"Baz."

"Yes, *Baz*." Maria glanced at James. "Your condition led us to his activities. We traced the skull in question to the 32d century, to the period when the Kane Foundation was being set up. We translated back to that time and encountered Baz, who was engaged in secret temporal experiments. Unfortunately, we underestimated him."

"You certainly did, didn't you?" I said. "He stole one of your TDDs."

"We'll get it back from him," said James.

"That doesn't really matter, does it?" I said. "Baz said it didn't work properly. He'll probably get stuck sometime and you can go and get him."

James cleared his throat. "That TDD is in perfect working order. It is also self-energizing, somewhat like a sol-shot deprived of sunlight."

"It certainly made me feel bad," I said. "And Baz couldn't control it properly."

"Our TDDs work by converting human energy," said Maria. "Proper training is necessary to stabilize them. No doubt Baz allowed it to convert your energy as well as his own."

"And I didn't have much to convert," I said sourly.

"So," said Maria, "we have to find Baz and get that TDD or we could have multiple anomalies."

"You'll have your work cut out," I said. "He's hopping around collecting memorabilia. Or so he said."

Maria sighed. "We'll have to start our research all over again. Since we removed you from your critical period, the time scheme has probably been changed."

"Why didn't you just let me die?" I asked.

"It was a matter of deciding which anomaly was less injurious," said Maria. "A death from nerve-burn before that condition should have been possible was only a minor factor, but the implications could have been large."

They certainly would have been large to me!

"I guess you could always go back and catch Baz in the mall," I said.

"Unfortunately, that would undo your recovery," said Maria. "No, if we decide to replace you in your own time scheme, dead or alive, we'll have to try to intercept Baz at a later period."

The Other Option

"Dead or alive? *If* you decide to return me?"

"Please understand, Tom," said Maria, "if it were up to us, we'd take you home and consider it a job well done. But there are things that cannot be justified. The Kane Foundation exists to solve anomalies, but some things, though regrettable, are the products of their times and can't be changed."

"Like what?" I said.

"Like the extinction of *Cacatua galerita*," said James grumpily. "That *could* be changed if I were authorized to fetch some fresh DNA from the past, but will the Foundation allow it? No! They keep on citing natural causes!" He glowered at me. "I don't call it natural that people from your time and beyond destroyed the habitats of so many…"

"James," Maria warned.

Then Coxie spoke up. "*Cacatua galerita* is what Cracker is. Do you really mean there are no sulfur-crested cockatoos left? None at all?"

"None," said James crossly. "And of course all organic museum specimens had to be destroyed during the germ-purge of 3273. If I could get access to some fresh DNA, or even a feather, I could clone…"

"Stop it, James," said Maria. "In your case, Tom, no one could claim natural causes. Not when you were exposed to a danger from your future. I believe your death could be classified as anomalous to a high degree. The fact remains that if we reinsert you in your time scheme, we could create more anomalies. We must identify all implications before we decide."

"What if you can't put me back?" I said.

"We would offer you a permanent home with us," said Maria.

"I want to go home."

"Believe me, Tom," said Maria, "we'd like to solve all the problems of the ages, but it can't be done. Our only job is to solve the anomalies brought about by the existence of time travel, and to do it with the least possible disturbance to the fabric of time."

"You'd better stop Baz then," I said. "It's your fault he's got the TDD."

Maria glanced at James. "It could be argued that the whole loop involving Baz is a recent anomaly," she said.

"We might not have found that without Tom. And since James and I intercepted you, Tom, we bear responsibility for any consequences. However, it still might be best if you remain with us."

There was a short silence. "How about Coxie and Dr. Pennyfather?" I asked.

"There's no problem with returning them to their own time scheme," said Maria, "subject to a thorough debriefing, of course."

Coxie looked relieved, but that didn't help me.

"Listen," I said. "I think I have a deal for you."

"It isn't ethical to bargain with a future," said Maria.

"Ethical or not, I have a plan," I said. "How's this? Baz is a much worse danger than I'd ever be. He has Lizba's time medallions, but they won't work. He also has Lizba's skull, the TDD, and the sol-shot. At this moment, he's on his way to get the medallions from the time when they were still working."

"He could have gone to any time period though," objected Coxie. "To Lizba's or ours, or any time before."

"I know where and when he is," I said.

Maria looked interested.

"Baz took me with him to steal the skull and made me tell him where and when to get the medallions. He could have dumped me anywhere in time, so I told him what he wanted to know."

Maria groaned.

"But," I said, "I told him the wrong time and the wrong place. So if you want to catch up with him, you've only got to arrange to be there a few minutes before he is."

"When and where?" demanded Maria. She was young and seemed nice, but for a moment she reminded me of Dr. Pennyfather. Well, I'd learned a thing or two about dealing with bullies.

"This is where the deal comes in." I tried to sound firm, but my voice was shaking. "If I tell you this, you've got a shortcut to cleaning up the whole mess. But *if* I tell you this, you've got to put me back – with Coxie – cured, and no questions asked. We won't say anything about time travel or about you or your times. You know you can trust us! We kept Lizba's secret for more than a year."

Maria and James glanced at one another, then Maria nodded slowly. "That sounds fair," she said. "In fact, you have the makings of a real temporal investigator, Tom! Are you sure you don't want to join us?"

"I'm sure," I said. "There's just one other thing. What happens to Baz when you catch him?"

"We return him to his own time scheme," said Maria, "having first retained the stolen TDD, naturally."

"And that's it?" I said.

"We have no authority to punish him."

"Great!" I said. "You talk about making *me* stay in the future, but you can't punish Baz! That's just not good enough. Baz will be up to something else as soon as your backs are turned, and I don't want to spend the rest of my life – now that I've got one – watching my back."

"What do you suggest, Tom?" asked Maria politely.

"I'll tell you when you get him," I said.

Maria smiled. "It's a deal. You tell us when and where to apprehend Baz."

I told them.

They took Coxie and me along, but they left Dr. Pennyfather in the isolation zone of the Kane Foundation. Boy, was she mad! The whole operation went like a dream, especially for me. I can't tell you how good it felt to be healthy again! We went back to the date and place I'd given Baz, but an hour earlier. Maria and James got us into the house. (Since it was a weekday, no one was home.) James planted a pair of fake medallions in a dresser, and then we waited.

Baz showed up and found the medallions. While he was busy gloating, Maria hit him with a little blast from a sol-shot. Baz crumpled like a wet tissue, James got his TDD back, and we all went back to the Kane Foundation.

Baz was not a happy time traveler, and pretty soon he wasn't a time traveler at all.

"What happens to me now?" Baz asked, more or less the way I had.

"You should be debriefed and returned to your own time," said Maria. "However, I believe Tom has some ideas for your future, so we'll listen to him first."

Baz looked at me with a big grin, but I could tell he was uneasy.

"You ought to recruit him," I said. "Make him one of your research experts. He's good at finding things out, aren't you, Baz? Of course, he'd have to be based at the Foundation all the time."

They couldn't do it just like that. They had to check their records to find out what Baz had been doing in his own future. It turned out he'd disappeared soon after Lizba and Palmer had, so Maria and James *did* recruit him on the grounds that they obviously already *had* recruited him. Weird, but sometimes time travel's a weird business, and if I were James and Maria, I'd never let Baz out of my sight. It sounds risky to let him work for the Foundation, but one thing you can bet: he'll never get his hands on another TDD.

Lucky Old James

There were just a few things left to sort out. First, there were the time medallions. They were ruined, and James put them in the Foundation museum for safekeeping. Check.

Then, there was the sol-shot. Maria took that away from Baz, and it went into the museum, too. Check.

Dr. Pennyfather wanted to get into the museum, but James locked her out. It did my heart good to see Dr. Pennyfather getting a taste of her own medicine. She also wanted to come on the next trip, but James wouldn't let her do that, either. She wanted to know everything about Kane and the Kane Foundation. For some reason, she seemed really interested in Kane! James wouldn't tell her anything at all. Check and double-check.

I was beginning to like James, so I decided to leave him a present when we left. I had just the thing...

The last problem was what to do with Lizba's skull. James and Maria decided that it didn't belong in the museum. They couldn't let Dr. Pennyfather keep it, so in the end we went to the Asbestos Ranges, and then came back to the present. We climbed the hill, and James very carefully dug up a small tree. He buried the skull in the hole and replanted the tree.

"Rest in peace, Lizba," I said.

"Yes," said Coxie. "Rest in peace."

Then we all went down the hill again. On the way, we saw (and heard) a flock of sulfur-crested cockatoos, squawking and shrieking like a hundred Crackers. James looked up wistfully. "*Cacatua galerita,*" he said. "Aren't they wonderful? What I wouldn't give for..."

"Don't even think about it," said Maria. "We're here to solve anomalies, not to create them."

Finally, we went back for Dr. Pennyfather. She was *really* mad at being kept out of things. She wanted the skull back. She wanted exact details on my treatment and on the workings of time travel and the development of the human race. She wanted to be taken back to the 10th century and the 1st century and to prehistoric times.

"Take her," advised Coxie. "Maybe she'll be eaten by a dinosaur."

She *also* wanted to witness the beginning of human life and to see the 50th century. She wanted to interview Kane. She wanted a hundred other things, too. I'm happy to report that she didn't get a single one of them. What she *did* get was a long lecture from James and the threat of having her memory vacuumed.

That shut her up.

We sorted out the final details of our story, and then we were ready to roll. At the last minute, I slipped quickly into the museum and left the present for James on the counter, then we left the Foundation and were zipped back to our own time.

There was a sort of blink, and then I was lying in the ambulance, and an ambulance attendant was peering at me closely. "What's up?" I yelled, and sat up.

I tried to talk the attendants into letting me out of the ambulance, but no such luck. They carted me off to the hospital, then stuck me in the intensive care unit. Mom and Dad came, and tried to find out what was going on, but nobody could explain. The ambulance attendant swore I'd stopped breathing, but every test proved that I was perfectly fit. All the same, they kept me in for another day just to make sure. Coxie came to visit. We were eating our way through a big bunch of grapes when we heard a tapping sound at the door.

"Coxie, tell me it isn't who I think it is," I said.

"It is," said Coxie.

I laid down flat and folded my hands on my chest. "Tell her I've died."

Too late. Dr. Pennyfather was already by the bed. "Hello, boys."

We stared at her because there was something wrong with her voice. And something wrong with her face. She was trying to smile, I think.

"We have some matters to discuss, don't we, boys?" Out came three big notebooks, and I groaned. "First of all," she said, in a too sweet voice, "I must ask you to relate your own separate impressions of the future. Write down whatever you can remember. Don't discuss it beforehand, just write down whatever you recall. I shall do the same, and we'll compare the three accounts." She smiled again. "You are very privileged to be a part of this. Your help will be of immeasurable value to my paper."

Coxie and I glanced at one another, and I gave him a little nod.

"What paper, Dr. Pennyfather?" he asked.

"My paper on temporal translation, and on the Kane Foundation," said Dr. Pennyfather. "Physical evidence is lacking, but there *are* your test results, Tom. You are now fully recovered from your nerve-burn."

"My what?" I said.

"Your nerve-burn," repeated Dr. Pennyfather.

Coxie and I shrugged. "I don't know anything about that, Dr. Pennyfather," I said. "But thanks for coming in. And thanks for calling the ambulance. Apparently I nearly choked on something. Good thing you were there, right?"

Dr. Pennyfather's smile slipped. "I don't know what you two are up to, but I insist that you write those accounts now. I want every detail from the past weeks. Every detail you remember from the 35th century."

I laughed. "This is the 20th century, not the 35th. What are you talking about?"

Dr. Pennyfather practically ground her teeth. "I want to know everything about Dr. Smith and his mother, about

121

that insufferable James and Maria and the Kane Foundation, about time travel and its relationship to the opalized skull, and about nerve-burn and its causes and treatment. You must cooperate."

Coxie and I looked at her blankly. "What *is* she talking about?" I said to Coxie.

Dr. Pennyfather was really teed off, but there was really nothing she could do. She did try to get Sergeant Kerry to question me again about the theft of the skull, but after she started babbling about time travel, medallions, and ray guns, they dropped the whole case. Later, we heard the university had let her go, on the grounds that her theories were unsound. I bet they'd been waiting for an excuse to do that for ages! These days, I hear she's working on the preservation of flora and fauna and writing science fiction. She's also gotten married to some poor man. Oddly enough, his surname is Kane...

All this happened some time ago. For months, I used to jump every time a light flickered or a stranger looked at me, but now I've decided that it really is all over. By the end of the summer I'd grown a lot, and now I'm almost bigger than Dad.

Sometimes I think about James and Maria and Baz. Sometimes I remember Lizba. I don't know exactly where her skull is buried, because the Asbestos Ranges are so vast and it was dark when we were there. But still, it's there in the hills where she died, with a healthy little tree standing guard. And James and Maria are (will be) doing their best to keep time safe from people like Baz. I think that's what Lizba would have liked.

The other day, I was at Coxie's place. His sister the Noise Machine was pretending to be a jet plane, so Coxie and I were out in the parrot palace with Cracker and his new friend Jojo to get some peace. Cracker was swinging wildly on his perch, shrieking and showing off, and Jojo was cuddling up under Coxie's chin and chattering.

"Poor old James," said Coxie, out of the blue.

That was all he said, but I knew what he meant. "Hey Coxie," I said. "What would you say if I told you one of Cracker's feathers had somehow found its way into the 35th century?"

A big smile spread over Coxie's face. "Feathers carry DNA, don't they?" he said.

"Yes. A whole sulfur-crested cockatoo blueprint in one little white package. Hard to believe, right?"

"Yes," said Coxie. "It's hard to believe." He put Jojo back on the perch, and Cracker jumped down to nibble on Coxie's ear.

"So, what would you say?" I asked.

"I'd say, lucky old James," said Coxie.

Timeline

3570 B.C.	Lizba Smith dies and the last set of time-travel medallions are destroyed.
3000 B.C.	Tom and Coxie meet Lizba, and Tom is shot with a sol-shot.
A.D. 1700	Baz and Tom visit the site of Dr. Pennyfather's future home.
A.D. 1990s	The active time scheme. Tom and Coxie have the adventures related in *Timedetectors*. For adventures related in *A Theft in Time: Timedetectors II,* please see Magnified Timeline.
A.D. 3149	The sol-shot is invented.
A.D. 3151	The first case of nerve-burn is diagnosed.
A.D. 3152	Lizba Smith is born.
A.D. 3155	Kane, founder of the Kane Foundation, is born.
A.D. 3160	Palmer, Lizba's partner in the creation of the time medallions, dies.
A.D. 3193	The original time medallions are destroyed.
A.D. 3195	Baz experiments with creating time travel. The Kane Foundation is established.
A.D. 3201	Time-Displacement Devices (TDDs) are developed.
A.D. 3273	The germ-purge, in which the last specimens of *Cacatua galerita* are destroyed, is carried out.
A.D. 3430	James is born.
A.D. 3432	Maria is born.
A.D. 3453	Tom arrives in the future to be treated for nerve-burn.

Magnified Timeline

A.D. 1700   Baz and Tom visit the site of Dr. Pennyfather's future home.

A.D. 1990s   The active time scheme.

                   May 3, 199_, eighteen months before Day One.
                   James, Maria, Tom, and Coxie set a trap for Baz.

Day One   Tom telephones Sergeant Kerry in an attempt to find the skull. Tom writes to Dr. Pennyfather, requesting a meeting with her.

Day Nine   Baz and Tom enter Dr. Pennyfather's house after traveling to 1700 in order to break in.

Day Eleven   Tom arrives in Devonport.
                   9:00 A.M.   Tom arrives at Dr. Pennyfather's house.
                   9:30 A.M.   Tom leaves Dr. Pennyfather's house and is shadowed by Baz through the mall.
                   9:45 A.M.   Tom arrives at Coxie's house.
                   12:00 P.M. Tom and Coxie meet Baz at the mall.
                   3:00 P.M.   Tom, Coxie, and Baz visit Dr. Pennyfather's house.
                   5:00 P.M.   Tom and Coxie return to Coxie's. Tom is questioned by Sergeant Kerry.
                   7:00 P.M.   Tom and Coxie go to a movie.
                   7:45 P.M.   Dr. Pennyfather questions Tom in the lobby of the movie theater.
                   9:00 P.M.   Tom and Coxie leave the movie theater and are chased by James and Maria. Baz appears and kidnaps Tom.
                   9:45 P.M.   Tom is left by Baz and collapses. Tom is taken into the future to be treated for nerve-burn.
                   11:30 P.M. Tom is taken to the hospital, and his parents visit.

Day Twelve   Dr. Pennyfather and Coxie visit Tom in the hospital.

A.D. 3453   Tom arrives in the future to be treated for nerve-burn.

From the Authors

We live in Tasmania with our two children, and our entire family loves a good science fiction story. At the end of our first time-travel adventure, *Timedetectors*, our heroes, Tom and Coxie, were left with a futuristic ray gun that no longer worked. What would happen, we wondered, if the weapon mysteriously recharged? Or if someone in the future decided the boys knew too much? We wrote *A Theft in Time* to find out.

Darrel and Sally Odgers

From the Illustrator

I grew up with one ambition – to be an artist. After I finished school, I started my first job, which was drawing boots and clothing for a surplus supply store. From there, I went on to drawing comic strips and illustrating and designing T-shirts and blankets. Finally, I began painting and illustrating children's books, which I have been doing for the past six years.

Richard Hoit

Written by **Darrel** and **Sally Odgers**
Illustrated by **Richard Hoit**
Edited by **David Nuss**
Designed by **Pat Madorin**

04 03 02 01 00 99
11 10 9 8 7 6 5 4 3 2

Distributed in the United States of America by
    Rigby
    a division of Reed Elsevier Inc.
    P.O. Box 797
    Crystal Lake, IL 60039-0797

Printed by Colorcraft, Hong Kong
ISBN: 1-57257-678-2

A Theft in Time:
Timedetectors II

Tom and Coxie thought they had put
time travel behind them. But when
Tom becomes ill and his search for a
missing skull leads him to team up
with Coxie again, the past and the
future are placed very much in doubt.
Then, a mysterious stranger from the
future begins to follow them, and a
pesky doctor accuses Tom of stealing
the very skull he has been hoping to
find. But when two more strangers
appear from the future and try to
grab Tom and Coxie, the boys don't
know where to turn. What's more,
Tom is getting sicker and sicker, and
time seems to be running out...

Rigby

ISBN: 1-57257-678-2

SO-BEI-745